GCSE MANUFACTURING

Steve Cushing

Hodder & Stoughton

A MEMBER OF THE HODDER HEADLINE GROUP

Orders: please contact Bookpoint Ltd, 130 Milton Park, Abingdon, Oxon OX14 4SB. Telephone: (44) 01235 827720.
Fax: (44) 01235 400454. Lines are open from 9.00–6.00, Monday to Saturday, with a 24-hour message answering service.
You can also order through our website **www.hodderheadline.co.uk**.

British Library Cataloguing in Publication Data
A catalogue record for this title is available from the British Library

ISBN 0 340 81409 8

This edition published 2004

Impression number   10 9 8 7 6 5 4 3 2 1

Year   2007 2006 2005 2004

Copyright © Steve Cushing 2004

Cover photo from Rosenfeld Images Ltd/Science Photo Library

Typeset by Phoenix Photosetting, Chatham, Kent

Printed in Great Britain for Hodder & Stoughton Educational, a division of Hodder Headline Plc, 338 Euston Road, London NW1 3BH by J.W. Arrowsmith Ltd., Bristol

Acknowledgements

The author would like to thank Nyree Williams for her support and input, and Diana Spencer and James de Winter for assisting with the content.

The publishers would like to thank the following individuals and institutions for permission to reproduce copyright material:

© ACESTOCK.COM – 2.3; © Action Plus – 2.2c; © Alex Segre/REX – 1.4; © Alinari Archives/CORBIS – 1.33; © ANDANSON JAMES/CORBIS SYGMA – 1.3; © Bernard Annebicque/CORBIS SYGMA – 1.30, 3.6; © B.D.I. Images – 1.8, 1.9, 1.10, 1.18, 1.47, 3.5; © Bill Varie/CORBIS – 2.7; © Brownie Harris/CORBIS – 3.1; © Charles O'Rear/CORBIS – 1.13, 2.4, 3.16; © CORBIS – 1.21b, 1.29, 1.44, 2.2a, 3.4; © Craig Aurness/CORBIS – 3.12; © Dave Bartruff/CORBIS – 1.5; © David Butow/CORBIS – 1.19; © Don Mason/CORBIS – 1.28, 2.15; © Ed Kashi/CORBIS – 2.16; © Edifice Photo – 1.20; © Firefly Productions/CORBIS – 2.6; © Gary Braasch/CORBIS – 1.43; © James Marshall/CORBIS – 1.25; © Jean Heguy/CORBIS – 1.21a; © Jose Luis Pelaez, Inc./CORBIS – 1.31; © Kevin Wilton; Eye Ubiquitous/CORBIS – 2.8; © L. Clarke/CORBIS – 3.19; © Macduff Everton/CORBIS -1.40; © Michael S. Yamashita/CORBIS – 3.20; © NASA/Roger Ressmeyer/CORBIS – 3.9; © Paul A. Souders/CORBIS – 1.42; © Peggy & Ronald Barnett/CORBIS – 1.26; © Peter Vadnai/CORBIS – 3.3; © REDFERNS Music Picture Library – 1.15a, 1.15b, 2.2b; © Reuters/CORBIS – 1.2a, 1.35; © Richard T. Nowitz/CORBIS – 1.6; © Scott Olson/Getty Images – 1.2b; © Simon Bruty/SI/NewSport/Corbis – 3.22b; © Steve Chenn/CORBIS – 1.32, 3.7; © Still Pictures – 1.23; © Ted Horowitz/CORBIS – 1.24; © Terry W. Eggers/CORBIS – 3.13; © The Sage Gateshead, Photographer: Nigel Young, Architect: Foster and Partners – 1.34 and 1.48; © Tom Wagner/CORBIS SABA – 1.16; © 2004 TopFoto – 1.14, 1.17, 1.46, 2.9; © VANDER ZWALM DAN/CORBIS SYGMA – 1.11; © Volkswagen – 1.7.

Internal artwork by Daedalus Studios and Barking Dog Art.

Every effort has been made to obtain necessary permission with reference to copyright material. The publishers apologise if inadvertently any sources remain unacknowledged and will be glad to make the necessary arrangements at the earliest opportunity.

Contents

GCSE Manufacturing

Introduction

This book has been written for students studying for the Applied GCSE in Manufacturing. It aims to help and support them in all aspects of the course, providing advice on both practical and theoretical areas of the specification.

Applied GCSE courses are intended to be vocational in nature and are double awards. That means that they are worth two GCSEs rather than one. The Applied GCSE in Manufacturing focuses on the practical aspects of manufacturing design and production.

The vocational nature of the course means that the emphasis for assessment is on practical work, presented as a portfolio of evidence. The evidence must be related to real-life problems, such as how to package a fragile food product so that it gets to the customer in perfect condition. If possible, this evidence should be based on a real organisation that the student can visit to see the manufacturing process and discuss production requirements. If this is not possible, teachers will need to ensure that the student has sufficient case study material to guarantee that the task is realistic and challenging.

Visits to a wide range of manufacturing companies should form an important method of studying for this course. No amount of classroom activity can replace the experience gained from seeing real products being made and packaged. It is exciting and interesting to see manufacturing in action, and visits will provide an element of careers guidance as well as vital background information for the GCSE course. It is hard for any student to imagine the range of career opportunities available in manufacturing without actually seeing what goes on in real life. Design and drafting, procurement and production planning, quality control and testing are roles that students might want to consider in the future, as well as practical skill areas such as food production or component machining.

This book is divided into three main sections:

Chapter 1 focuses on Unit 1 of the GCSE specification. It aims to help students understand a design brief and draw up a specification. Students need to carry out investigations, and this chapter will help them plan their investigations and apply their skills, knowledge and understanding to the manufacturing problem they are considering. The examples in the book can be used to develop skills and knowledge and provide a starting point for their real-life investigation, so that when they visit a real manufacturing company they are well prepared for what they will find. The activities will provide a practical focus for this important task, and the examples of workshop drawings and design briefs will give an indication of what the student is expected to do.

Chapter 2 explores the production methods used in manufacturing, and covers Unit 2 of the GCSE specification. It explains the importance of quality control standards and the skills and techniques needed to meet those standards. Basic skills, tools and techniques are covered to provide a foundation for understanding the production of manufacturing products. The section on health and safety covers regulations and the way they are applied in practical terms through risk assessments and safety procedures. Hygiene requirements are also considered.

Chapter 3 covers the use of new technology in the world of manufacturing, Unit 3 of the specification. It looks at new materials, production methods and environmental considerations. As this unit is assessed by an external test, it provides revision notes and practice questions. It is important that students carry out their own research into these exciting areas, which are constantly changing. Clear notes will make revising for the examination much easier. Students will also find information for this unit as they build up their portfolio. Taking notes as they go along will help build the knowledge needed for the examination and will give them a greater understanding of the process under discussion.

Building Your Portfolio

The practical work that forms such a vital part of this course needs to be supported by a portfolio of evidence. Students need to understand how to present evidence that demonstrates all aspects of the design and production process.

The portfolio should only contain the evidence required by the assessment evidence grid, and should be kept separately from class notes. The evidence required for each individual unit should be filed in separate and complete sections of the portfolio.

Work should be presented in an organised way that is easy to follow. Each section should be labelled, and each piece of work should have a heading to provide a clear indication of what the page is intended to demonstrate. The sections should follow the assessment grid closely so that it is easy to check that all areas have been covered.

The portfolio should include a table of contents and all pages should be numbered. Students should include their name and centre number on each page, and candidate number if possible. The portfolio should contain drawings and photographs to illustrate the progress of the work, and these should be annotated to show exactly how the product was produced and what tools and techniques were involved. Any problems met along the way should be described, together with how they were solved.

Designing Products for Manufacture

1

CHAPTER AIMS & INTRODUCTION

This chapter will explore:

- product requirements and constraints
- materials, their properties, availability, performance and constraints
- designing a product
- scientific principles
- presenting design ideas and designs
- marketing a product
- product quality, performance and cost
- health, safety and hygiene
- materials handling and storage
- packaging
- production planning.

This chapter of the book covers the first part of the design process. It discusses the information that should be in a design brief, and the specifications that should be developed from the brief. Turning a specification into a design takes planning and research, and this chapter covers the research and investigation required as part of the planning process.

Section 1 contains a lot of information about planning. It is very tempting to rush in and make something. However, badly-planned products have a habit of going wrong. A little more thinking time will help to sort out potential difficulties so that production can run more smoothly.

There is a section on types of drawing – these need practice, but they then become a designer's most valuable tool in defining and presenting a product.

Computers can be used throughout the design and production process, from drawing up project schedules to manipulating images or carrying out strength calculations.

1 PRODUCT REQUIREMENTS AND CONSTRAINTS

A designer's work is important. Any decision made by the designer potentially affects an entire product, and the company's reputation and bank balance. Any mistakes can render a design completely useless and require time-consuming corrections. A good designer has to know the right steps and, even more importantly, the wrong steps, in order to develop a product from a set of constraints.

All designs are trade-offs between the ideal and the possible. Designers will receive a set of design criteria that will balance a number of factors, similar to those listed below for a car. We will explore this in more detail in later sections of the book.

Finances

When a manufacturing company decides to produce a product it has first to consider its finances. Finances is the term businesses use to refer to the management of money. Money is one of the most important inputs to any manufacturing business. If the manufacturer does not have existing buildings and equipment, start-up costs can be very expensive. Most products are made by existing companies with equipment and buildings. Each step must be costed as the manufacturer will need to pay out this money before having anything to sell.

The finance department will be responsible for:

* working out how much money is needed for each stage
* drawing up a budget plan and cash flow
* obtaining the necessary money through loans or other sources
* spending the money as identified in the plan
* reporting on the financial condition of the project.

Criterion	Trade-off decisions
Function	Number of passengers, size, speed, economy, type of engine
Form	Sports car, off-road vehicle
Quality standards	High quality/high cost, low quality/low cost
Styling (aesthetics)	Styling, colours, shape
Market	Upper middle-class, working-class
Standardization	Use of existing parts, e.g. engine, wheels, lights
Durability	How reliable, how much time between services
Time-scales	Available this year, next year, in 10 years' time
Size of market	Large market/large sales, small market/small sales
Scope of accessories	Range of alternatives at extra cost

Table 1.1 Design criteria and decision factors for designing a car

Steps in Undertaking a Project

All projects are developed over time and certain stages take place before others. Often one project leads directly to another. Each step within the production process forms part of a production cycle.

1. Start-up – meetings to develop a feel for the product, to identify its requirements and constraints.

2. Concept – develop a rough model (or models) that includes all the major features of the final design and prove that it meets the requirements set in step 1. Then make the final decision.

3. Design – production of the full design, splitting the concept into required parts, etc. Compiling the final design and checking that it meets the requirements.

4. Detailed design – working out any problems from step 3 and producing all the required documents (i.e. drawings).

5. Manufacture – instructions are passed to the manufacturer. The designer and the manufacturer will still need to be in touch to deal with any problems that may arise.

Time As an Input

One of the things people often forget when considering manufacturing inputs is the importance of time. Time costs money. Calculating the time it will take to make something and whether it is cost efficient is a vital part of any manufacturing process. Most sports people train themselves to be efficient in terms of time. Runners, swimmers, skiers and cyclists all race against the clock and they do this by trying to be as efficient as they can. A manufacturer has to do the same thing. If you were running in a relay race you would want the best people you could get for each stage of the race. A manufacturer needs the best processes and people at each stage of the process.

They need to calculate how much time it will take to complete each stage of manufacture. Manufacturers call the measurement of work 'time study' or 'work measurement'. In order to measure work efficiency, and out-sell their competitors, manufacturers use a number of methods to measure the efficiency of both processes and workers. This can range from the use of a stop watch to automated time measurement systems and work sampling.

Personnel or Support

If more than one person is involved in the manufacture of a product it is important to define their tasks rigidly, along with their responsibilities and to whom they are accountable. If they are going to be making decisions that will affect other people's work, it is important to set a standard of communication between the members of the team. A good method of communication is through the concept model. The concept model is broken into parts and each person is assigned a chunk. They can alter whatever they want (within constraints) except for the interface of the part within the master model. They must check the master regularly to ensure their part conforms to the master model.

ACTIVITIES

1. Imagine you are going to manufacture a product one of your friends has designed. What questions would you ask to ensure you produced exactly what he or she had in mind?

2. What problems would companies have if the manufacturers did not liaise with the designers and simply made what they felt was best? Bear in mind the designer has already worked from a brief.

PORTFOLIO NOTES

Explore the costs involved in each stage of manufacture.

List a set of trade-offs for your chosen product.

2 THE DESIGN BRIEF

Function

Form follows function

Bauhaus, Germany 1932

If you ask the questions, What is this for? and What does it have to do? you will be getting close to the function of the product. Function is really about just that, what is it meant to do and where? However, products often need to be more than functional and we always need to bear that in mind when producing goods. Aesthetics (how good the product looks) may also be important.

Fig 1.2a This jeep is an example of a purely functional vehicle

Fig 1.2b This vehicle features many non-functional accessories

In order for a manufactured product to function properly the designers need to know the following:

- who will use it?
- where will it be used?
- what will it have to endure?
- what should it do well?

From the answers to these questions you can start to narrow down your design brief. Decisions like which materials to use will start to become more obvious, because you can start to reject some as unsuitable.

The functions of a waterproof jacket mean that:

- it needs to be waterproof
- it must be the right shape and size
- it will resist rain for a long time.

If it fails on any of these issues or more then it is not functional and will not succeed.

A simple formula is that if the product is functional it works well! You only tend to notice products that are not functional, i.e. do not work well.

ACTIVITIES

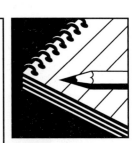

1. Sometimes the function of a manufactured product is not so obvious. For instance, a mass produced sweet's main function is to taste good, but what else about it helps it function well?

2. Make a list of the functions of your favourite footwear. They may not be as obvious as you think; aesthetics may be a priority, and this then starts to confuse things!

KEY WORDS

Form   how the product looks, the shape of the product

Function   the job the product has to do

Aesthetics   the way a product looks and feels, and the way it makes us feel when we look at it

PORTFOLIO NOTES

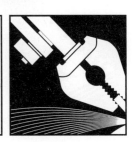

Include a list of the functions your product has to perform.

Show your designs to other people and see how they react to the appearance of your product, then record these opinions.

Performance

The word performance in the context of a manufactured product refers to how well the product works. If we talk about the performance of wall paint, we would consider things like how long it will last before flaking, whether the colour fades quickly, how easy it is to apply and so on.

The performance of an engine part is the same, but it works in a completely different environment. In this context you will need to know exactly what materials will survive cold, extreme heat, friction, chemical attacks, vibration, and so on. So in order to ensure the best performance of your product you really need to know your materials and the environment in which the product will be used.

Fig 1.3 A chef will use their favourite pan

A chef may have a favourite pan for a particular dish because that pan works best. It performs well, it may spread heat evenly, hold the contents well or be light yet strong. All of these things are difficult to test before a model or prototype is made. Yet the performance of a product is essential to its success. A product that does its job but does not do it as well as another product will not sell well.

Sometimes we have to put up with a product that does not perform as well as another because of cost, or other factors. When two products cost similar amounts and they are aimed at the same market, performance really matters.

Some products perform very well in some areas, but not so well in others. Customers will often try to find a product that works well in everything it is meant to do, but sometimes this is an unrealistic expectation. Washer dryers, for example, could be very good at washing or drying, but they are rarely as good as separate washing machines and tumble dryers.

In these situations a compromise may be decided upon – the washer dryer takes up less space and the clothes do not need to be removed after washing and put into a dryer. So the less efficient product has other benefits that may appeal to customers.

ACTIVITIES

1. Take any pen you have that you think is good at what it does and list why you think it performs well. Does it last a long time? Is it comfortable to use? Does the ink flow well?

2. Sports clothes need to perform well: they may 'breathe' so that you do not sweat so much, they may be light or waterproof. What do you think would make an item of sports clothing perform well?

KEY WORDS

Performance   how well the product does the jobs it has to do

Environment   the surroundings the product has to work in

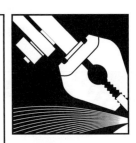

PORTFOLIO NOTES

You should include a list of performance criteria. These are ways of judging if your product is performing well.

As far as possible, performance criteria should be measurable. It is better to say, 'The product must cook in under 30 minutes' rather than 'The product must cook quickly'. You can then evaluate the performance of your finished product against these criteria.

Intended Markets

The word market in this context means the group or groups of people your product is intended for. Manufacturers will spend a lot of time on market research, probably before they even commission a designer, to see if there is a market for their products. They need to see if there is a demand for what they intend to make. If they get this wrong, then they may find no one buys their products, which in turn means they lose money.

Market researchers will often:

- interview people that they think may buy the product

- look at products around at the moment that do similar jobs

- compare the prices of existing products that are similar

- take apart similar products to find out how they were manufactured and how much they cost to manufacture. This is called disassembling or reverse engineering.

Once the product has been made, the marketing people then promote the product to the right audience. They will already have a profile of potential

Fig 1.4 These shoppers represent a particular market that can be targeted

customers and will try to advertise the product in magazines, TV shows and places that these customers will see. Manufacturers would not spend huge amounts of money advertising a designer watch in a child's comic because the market is wrong; they may well advertise sweets or games in the comic because the market is right. Advertising is a very powerful tool for manufacturers to communicate their ideas and show their products to the people they think will buy them.

There are often claims that certain forms of advertising should be banned – tobacco advertising for example.

Sometimes people feel that certain advertisements should be removed because of sexist or racist implications.

Advertising may take different forms and use different media. Manufacturers advertise on TV and radio. They use posters, place adverts in magazines and newspapers, and sponsor sporting events so that their name becomes associated with something exciting like football or motor racing.

Some companies sponsor programmes that advertise toys, rather than producing adverts between programmes. These are often aimed at children, as they can use 'pester power' to get their parents to buy them the toy they have been watching.

ACTIVITIES

1. An international drinks company may use a number of different ways to advertise their products. Produce a report detailing what sort of media they use and what form the advertising takes.

2. Produce a list of products that are marketed for your age group or sex. Record how these products are marketed and how successful you think the advertising has been.

KEY WORDS

Market   the people you are trying to sell a product to

Marketing   the advertising and publicity that will make your product attractive to that market

Market research   to find out if there is a market for your product and who will buy it

Interview   ask people what they think of your product

Compare   look at other products on the market

Reverse engineering   taking other products apart to see how they are made

PORTFOLIO NOTES

You should show that you have looked at other products that are already being made, and that you can analyse their good and bad points. You should learn from other people's designs, not copy them.

You should always try to carry out market research if you can. Computer spreadsheets and databases can help you to analyse the results of research.

Quantity

If a manufacturer gets the quantity they produce wrong, they are in big trouble. Too many goods for the market will mean that the goods may not sell. The manufacturer will have paid to make the product, and will not get the money back from selling them.

This is how everything links together: if the marketing people give the wrong information to the manufacturer, too many products are made. This will cost money as the materials will be purchased, machinery used and workers paid to produce products that do not get sold. This could cause the company to be declared bankrupt because it has paid out a lot of money that it has not got back from sales.

If the marketing department gets the quantity wrong and demand is higher than expected then the manufacturer loses money too. Customers will go to other suppliers; people may want the goods but cannot get them. It is a balancing act that the manufacturer has to get just right in order to survive.

Some goods are seasonal so manufacturers may sell them at certain times of the year. Christmas decorations do not sell well in the summer, so manufacturers of these products need to be prepared and have the right quantity of goods ready for a short period of time each year. Ice cream manufacturers sell more in the hot months than in the winter. In both of these examples the companies manufacture their products all year round. Ice cream is more difficult than Christmas decorations in this respect, because it has a short shelf life. If it is not sold after a certain period of time it will not be fit to eat. Products that will go off after a certain period of time are called perishable.

All manufacturers have to consider how they will meet the demand in terms of quantity, while keeping their production cycles as smooth as possible. This may mean making products and then storing them for long periods.

Fig 1.5 A surplus of goods can be bad news for the manufacturer

This may turn into a problem of over-production. The goods may eventually sell but storing the goods is expensive and slows down cash flow because the money from the sales of the goods doesn't arrive until a long time after the money has been spent to make them. If money has to be paid at the beginning of the cycle for materials and equipment, and will not come in until the goods are sold, cash flow can be a problem. The company may need to borrow money to cover this.

ACTIVITIES

1. In the food industry, over-production can cause serious problems. Investigate how the fast food industry overcomes this problem.

2. The clothing industry suffers from over-production and fast seasonal turn around. Fashions change quickly. Investigate how clothing companies can reduce the possibility of having thousands of last season's coats left in the spring or summer.

KEY WORDS

Quantity   the number of products to be produced

Seasonal   products and materials that are only available at certain times of the year

Shelf Life   how long perishable products can be stored and still be useable

Cash Flow   the money that is exchanged within the product cycle

PORTFOLIO NOTES

Decide how many of your product you intend to make. Explain how this will affect your design and the methods you use.

Styling and Aesthetic Appearance

The way a product looks matters to us and affects the way we feel about it. This is called aesthetics. Things like colour, texture, shape and form all join together to give us an opinion about products. It doesn't matter if it is a cake, a plate of food, a car or a pair of jeans, if it doesn't look right we may not buy it.

Most products do the things they are supposed to well. What manufacturers then have to do is to appeal to our sense of aesthetics and change the appearance of the product. Many cars have similar platforms (chassis) but by changing the body styling, the car can then appeal to another market (group of people). The same platform can be the base for a coupé, cabriolet, saloon, hatchback and estate.

The same is true of many other products. The internal

workings of many mobile phones are very similar, yet each model is attractive to different groups of people. Trainers are another good example; the variations in styling (shapes, colours, texture, etc.) are all designed to make the product look good. All trainers do the same job – protect our feet – they are just packaged differently.

Aesthetics and fashion can be confusing. Fashion sometimes takes things we thought of as unattractive and transforms them into desirable products overnight. In the 1980s, it became popular to wear your jeans the wrong way around, so much so that some manufacturers started to make jeans that appeared to be on backwards but were actually the right way round.

Fig 1.6 Aesthetics are important!

Fig 1.7 Different body styling will appeal to different markets

ACTIVITIES

1. Can you think of any products that you would have happily worn two years ago but find unattractive now? Write down your thoughts on why this is.

2. Collect images of televisions. Rank them in order of aesthetics: why are some more attractive than others?

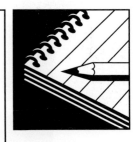

KEY WORDS

Aesthetics   the way a product looks and feels
Styling   the way a basic product can be changed to make it look different

PORTFOLIO NOTES

Make sketches of your basic product design with different types of styling and finish; for instance, different paint finishes, a different shape of button or an oval pie rather than a round one.

Quality Standards

The quality of a product will influence potential customers. If a product looks shabby or performs poorly because it is not put together well, it will only sell once, as customers will not buy it again. It is important to ensure that all products are well made and of good quality in terms of materials, construction, and how long they will last.

Every product that is produced must reach certain standards of quality. This applies particularly to safety and hygiene. The laws on product safety are very strict; manufacturers are fined a lot of money if they do not comply. Food standards are rigidly enforced, both at the place of manufacture, and at the point of sale.

Manufacturers must follow the British Standards and European Community laws on quality. Manufacturers of engineering components have to meet inspection authority standards for their equipment. These cover such things as how thick materials have to be to withstand certain pressures.

Products made for children have to comply with regulations regarding the size of components. The choke test is carried out to check whether any parts could be small enough for a child to put in their mouth but big enough to make them choke. These regulations apply particularly to children under three years old. There are also regulations about the type of paint and glue that should be used on children's toys.

Often quality is dictated by costs, but there are certain quality standards that all products must meet.

Fig 1.8 All food products should have a use by date

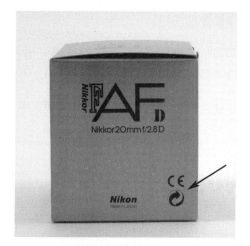

Fig 1.9 This symbol indicates the product has passed EU standards

ACTIVITY

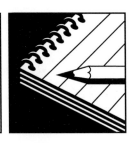

Look at a food package and see if you can find evidence of the standards that are maintained on that item.

KEY WORDS

Standards   rules that the product must follow

Regulations   laws that apply to the product

PORTFOLIO NOTES

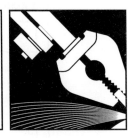

Try to find out about the British Standards that apply to your product. The Internet might help.

Costs

Before a product goes into production the total cost of the initial investment, material costs, labour costs, and distribution costs will be worked out. Each part or ingredient has to be carefully costed, as nothing is free. The manufacturer can then set a price that covers all of that plus a profit for themselves. This is the wholesale price that the shops can buy the product for.

Materials are usually bought in bulk. Buying large amounts of something can offer 'economies of scale'. This is the ability to buy at a low price per unit, because so many units are being purchased. The cost may be very small for a small ingredient of a single cake but on a run of a million cakes, for instance, this becomes very important.

The retailer (shop) will wish to make profit too. They set the final retail price, which is the price that you and I pay. Sometimes the manufacturer will set a recommended retail price (RRP) that they think the

product should be sold at, but that is only a recommendation. The retailer is free to set their own price, often lower than the RRP, as competition amongst retailers is often greater than among manufacturers. This means price of a product in one shop may be different to the price of the same product in another shop.

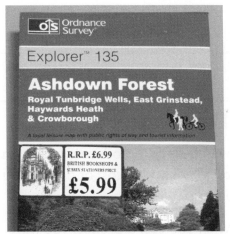

Fig 1.10 A product will often be sold at below the recommended retail price

The cost of a manufactured product may be made up of:

- materials
- production costs
- packaging
- advertising
- research and development costs
- distribution (often overseas).

Costs can be broken down into fixed costs and variable costs. A fixed cost will stay the same (remain fixed) however many products are produced. Fixed costs are something the manufacturer cannot alter without changing the manufacturing process or place of manufacture. A variable cost will go up and down (vary) with the quantity of products produced. It is something that may change over time or can be altered by changing aspects of the design.

Example:

Fixed costs £		Variable costs £	
Advertising	250	Labour	10 per hour
Distribution	150	Materials	30 per unit
Salaries	6000	Packaging	2 per unit
Tax	1000		
Electricity bill	800		
Specialist tools	4000		
Total	**12,200**		

The fixed costs add up to £12,200, and have to be paid whether any products are made or not.

If it takes two people one hour to make the product and they only make one, the variable cost will be:

2 people for 1 hour = 2 × 10		= £20
Materials and packaging		= £32
Making a total of		£52

Add on the fixed cost and the total is £12,252 for one product.

However if the company were to make 1000 in 20 hours using 10 workers, the fixed costs would remain the same, but the variable costs would be:

10 workers for 20 hours = 10 × 20 × 10		= £2000
Materials and packaging = 32 × 1000		= £32,000
Making a total of		£34,000

Add on the fixed cost and the total is £46,200.

But that is for 1000 products, so each product costs £46,200/1000 = £46.20.

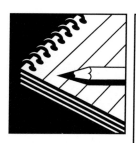

ACTIVITIES

1. Investigate and produce a report on the manufacturing cost of a simple product. You may find the cost of distributing and packing is far more than the product costs to make.

2. When you cost a product you have made or designed have a look at similar products and what they cost in the shops. Do they perform as well as yours might if it went into production? How much profit do you think the retailer has made?

KEY WORDS

Fixed costs   costs, such as electricity and staff salaries, which have to be paid each month

Variable costs   costs that change depending on how many products are being produced

Recommended retail price   the price a manufacturer suggests should be charged for a product

PORTFOLIO NOTES

Work out the cost of your product as accurately as you can. Look at the set up costs, and see how many products you would have to make to recover the set up costs.

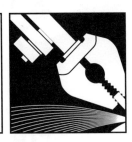

Timescales

To keep costs down and get the goods to the shops in time, managers need to keep a close eye on their production control systems. Production managers are keen to:

- reduce production timescales
- reduce production costs
- fix accurate manufacturing schedules
- monitor timescales
- produce a good quality product.

To do this, production managers need reliable information systems to help with:

- planning production times
- ordering raw material and component parts

- forecasting output and capacity for manufacturing machinery
- working out production costs.

Time is a considerable cost in manufacturing. The time taken to produce a product affects many of the costs of producing it.

A machine uses energy to make it work. The longer the machine is used for, the more energy it will need, and therefore the greater the fuel costs will be. The longer a product takes to manufacture the greater the hourly pay bill will be. It is therefore essential that timescales are carefully worked out.

You can plan the timescale for your product, just as a production manager in industry would have to. Keeping to your timescale means your work will be finished on time.

ACTIVITY

Investigate the timescale from the initial design brief to the mass production of a new car, house, or child's toy.

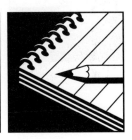

KEY WORDS

Timescale   the amount of time taken to produce a product

Schedule   a timetable to plan the amount of time needed for each stage of production

PORTFOLIO NOTES

If your designs really went into production what timescale would you give from the initial product design to delivering the product into the shops?

Draw up a plan for your own timescale and try to keep to it to make sure your project is finished on schedule.

Product Design Details

At the start of a project, designers will work with marketing and technical staff to make sure they know what the customer needs and how long they have to produce the goods. A functional specification is usually completed that states what the product has to do, what features it needs and how it should look and feel. It will identify the desired product capabilities such as performance requirements, features, functions, looks and feel.

At this stage a designer has to decide:

- what materials are to be used
- how the product is to be made

- how the product should perform
- what functions it should have
- how it will look aesthetically
- the product's size and shape
- how well it will meet the needs of the person who is to use it.

The process needs to be planned carefully and be clearly documented. Regular reports and quality checks need to be built in to the process. This should keep the product up to the standards set by the client and by industry. Detailed designs are essential if the final product is to meet its specification. If this is not done properly the product will probably fail in some or all of its functions.

ACTIVITIES

1. Look around the room you are in. List what you think the product design details are for the room.

2. What would the product design details be for a new flavour of crisps? Record your ideas as a report.

PORTFOLIO NOTES

Look at the list of things a designer has to decide. You, as a designer, have to decide these things for your product. You will need to document your decisions carefully.

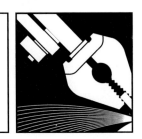

PRODUCTION DETAILS AND CONSTRAINTS ③

As a manufacturer, one of the important factors that you will need to consider is the most cost-effective and efficient way to manufacture your product. It does not matter if the product is a new sweet, drink or car – the same factors need to be considered. These might include the following.

- What are the properties and features of the materials and components that make them suitable for certain processes? Can they be bought in?

- What is the most appropriate technology for a particular process and material?

- When and where are health, safety and hygiene factors important in the production process?

- Quality standards required by the customer and/or the sector – is a special quality of material required?

- Are there enough staff? Do they have the right skills and training?

Researching how leading manufacturing companies run their production lines as cost-effectively as possible will help you to carry out a similar system for your own products.

Sometimes it is better for a manufacturer to buy in ready-made components as this is cheaper than

making them themselves. In your own work you may buy in motors, ready-mixed ingredients and other ready-made components. It is also sometimes cheaper to buy components and materials in large quantities (bulk) as discounts will sometimes be given by the supplier. Do not forget that the cost of anything purchased must be recovered when the product is sold so if you have lots of materials left over you will not make a profit.

All manufacturers try to improve productivity (how many items they produce in a specific time) while keeping production costs low. This creates a conflict. More machines and highly trained operatives would improve the amount of items produced in a given time, but the investment would raise production costs.

The best way to improve productivity is to reduce the 'product cycle time' – the time between the completion of one item and the completion of the next item. This is usually done by careful planning and sequencing of the production processes. For example, it may be possible to schedule a practical activity to be carried out on one item while another item is drying or baking. The example overleaf shows how finishes could be applied to a product; the first example has a long cycle time, the second example has a short cycle

Fig 1.11 Materials must be tested for their suitability

time, therefore the second example could help improve productivity.

Reducing the cycle time is not always possible, as the different operations may have to be carried out by specialists, or the equipment may be in use for other things. Manufacturers try to schedule work in this way for all products where a number of the same items are made.

Long production cycle

Item 1	Spray	Dry	Spray	Dry	Polish	Finished						
Item 2							Spray	Dry	Spray	Dry	Polish	Finished

Short production cycle

Item 1	Spray	Dry	Spray	Dry	Polish	Finished	
Item 2		Spray	Dry	Spray	Dry	Polish	Finished

Fig 1.12 An example of long and short production cycles

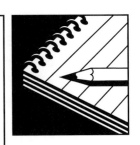

ACTIVITIES

1. Think about the ways in which large companies produce the same goods year after year to the same high standards. Take a typical chocolate bar or a battery as an example. How do you think they do this?

2. Try testing a friend and ask them what they think would be the production constraints for a wooden product, a plastic product and a tinned or chilled food product. Use the questions at the beginning of this section as a focus.

3. In carrying out practical activities, produce a timeline like the one in the example and see where time can be saved during production.

KEY WORDS

Cost-effective   the best price for a material or product

Materials   the things a product is made from

Components   the individual pieces that make up a product

Health, safety and hygiene   ways of working to make sure nobody gets hurt or becomes ill by making or using a product

Quality standards   rules that must be followed to produce a good quality product

Productivity   the number of components produced per day or per week

Investment   money that is put in to start up a project

Product cycle time   the amount of time it takes to make a product and start the next

Scheduling   organising the order in which things happen

PORTFOLIO NOTES

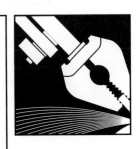

Make a list of the constraints that will affect your work. This may be a specialized piece of equipment that you do not have that would make the work easier, or a requirement from the customer to use a certain material that you feel is not ideal.

Produce a timeline like the one in the example and try to see where time can be saved during production.

Draw up a clear time plan for your work.

Labour

Henry Ford, the original owner and director of the Ford Motor Company, was known as the 'father of mass production lines'. He was the first industrialist to successfully develop the idea of a line of workers, each carrying out a specific task. Before this each person worked on all aspects of production.

For most industries, labour is the most costly part of the production process, so the manufacturing industry constantly tries to reduce its labour costs. Most manufacturers employ some skilled workers, who have had extensive training to do their job. They also employ some semi-skilled or unskilled workers, who have had far less training. Skilled workers usually get a higher rate of pay, but tend to be more flexible as they can do a wider range of tasks.

Over the last few decades, the manufacturing industry has tried to reduce its labour force by using automated production lines, robots and products that are designed to use fewer parts. New technology provides more and more alternatives to human labour. As old technology dies, new technology replaces it. New industries appear and grow. The IT industry which now employs many millions of workers, employed very few 30 years ago.

Poorly-trained workers are inefficient and often have low morale, which is why manufacturers are always encouraged to train workers to the highest

standards. This is easier for larger companies, as they tend to have better human resource facilities to do this.

Today skills are acquired in colleges or universities and are then developed through NVQs and similar qualifications before an individual starts work. Most people who work in manufacturing will have to update their skills many times during their working life, and have to be prepared to adapt to change.

Poorly-trained workers will produce badly made products or be unable to solve problems because they lack the skills to do so. Workers who are under pressure because they have to do too much will not perform as well.

Many companies try to save money by getting rid of staff. This immediately saves money by reducing the wages bill, but in the long term this can create major problems. The remaining staff may not be able to cope with the tasks they are set, through a lack of skills, or because they are too busy. Employing fewer members of staff is not always the most efficient way to save money.

Fig 1.13 An automated production line cuts down on manual labour

Fig 1.14 Women joined the manufacturing labour force during the Second World War

ACTIVITIES

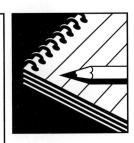

1. Describe three industries you think will become more automated in the next few years and explain why.

2. Describe the sort of jobs an unskilled worker could do in a factory that makes televisions. What would skilled workers do there?

KEY WORDS

Skills   the things that workers can do

Skilled   workers with a lot of training who can adapt their skills to many products

Semi-skilled   workers with some skills, but probably in one area of production

Unskilled   workers with just enough training to do simple jobs

Robots   computer-driven equipment that can do a job automatically

PORTFOLIO NOTES

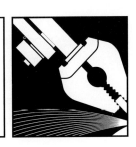

Look carefully at the processes you will use to create your product. Which of these processes do you think would need skilled workers to carry them out? Would any of them be suitable for robots to complete?

Quality of Material Components and Ingredients Used in Production

The quality of the materials that are used to produce an item depends on the price the retailer is expecting to charge for the item. High quality products tend to be produced using high quality materials. The markets that the products are aimed at dictate the quality of the ingredients, materials and components that go together to make the product.

The reason a particular musical instrument is more expensive than another almost identical instrument, is

Fig 1.15 Can you tell the difference between the Fender and the copy?

almost certainly because the materials used to make the instrument are of a higher quality or the product has been made by a more skilled or well-known manufacturer. This will probably produce an instrument that performs better.

Material buyers will be trained to look for special qualities in the material they are buying. A matured cheese for a pizza, for instance, will cost more than a mild cheese, but the mature cheese will have a stronger flavour. A denser weave in a fabric will take longer to make, use more yarn and therefore cost more. Sometimes high quality components must be used for safety reasons, such as with the parts of a medical monitoring device or surgical instrument.

Materials should be chosen because they are right for the function of the product, or the product will fail. For many products there are alternative materials that could be used, and manufacturers may change their choice of materials. For example, a new plastic may be developed that could replace another material. The new plastic may have a number of advantages over the previous material; it may be lighter, harder wearing or just cheaper.

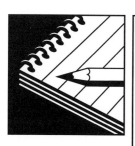

ACTIVITIES

1. Explain why people would be willing to pay more for one product, rather than a cheaper version that carries out similar tasks.

2. If a product fails because of poor quality components or material, what rights do customers have?

Available Technology

Manufacturers have to know and understand what production methods would be suitable. They have to balance the cost of using new technology for production purposes against the cost of using older equipment that may be unreliable, slow and possibly more labour-intensive.

New technology means that manufacturers can produce cheaper products. However, the new technology may cost the company a considerable amount of money. Some manufacturers rely on older technology and use the words 'traditionally made' or 'hand crafted' to sell their goods and suggest that modern technology was not used.

Deciding on the technology that suits a particular manufacturing process depends on the product that is being made. Some food production is still quite labour-intensive. The preparation of fresh salads for a supermarket, for instance, is still done by hand using low-paid workers. However, canning factories have been automated for some time.

Fiat proudly advertised in the 1980s that their cars were 'hand built by robots'. Robots make most cars and most of their components are produced on computer-controlled machines using CAM (computer-aided manufacturing). Virtual reality techniques can be used to model a new production line before it is constructed, so that expensive mistakes can be avoided.

Manufacturing companies invest a great deal of time and money in research and development. They research new technologies, such as materials and processes, which could be used to manufacture future products. Drug companies, for example, spend millions of pounds each year investigating the effects that drugs could have on a person before they will release a new drug for sale.

Fig 1.16 Workers hand-packing salads

ACTIVITIES

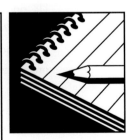

1. The clothing industry uses a combination of new and old technologies in the production of clothing. Carry out an investigation into a product and describe where each technology is used in the production process.

2. Look up the word technology in a dictionary or on the Internet and see what definitions you find.

PORTFOLIO NOTES

What technology could be used if your product was going to be put into a production process? Would investment in new technology be worthwhile?

Perhaps your product is deliberately low-tech. A hand-embroidered skirt should be advertised and marketed as hand-made and, therefore, no two items will be exactly the same.

Health, Safety and Hygiene During Production

Laws regulate how food is produced, and how products are manufactured in order to protect workers and consumers.

Hygiene is very important during the production process of foodstuffs, not only to prevent contamination but also to stop foreign bodies getting into the food. Strict rules must be adhered to throughout, regarding the surfaces used and the materials they are made from. Generally speaking most food production surfaces should be stainless steel, as it does not corrode and is easy to clean after each production run.

Noisy and dangerous environments mean that workers must protect their ears and wear safety helmets.

Any machine that cuts, crushes or rotates will have guards around it, and the machinery will not work unless the guards are in place.

The Health and Safety Executive (HSE) regulations and UK and EU laws on work safety are very clearly laid down. Any manufacturer that ignores them can lose a lot of money if it can be proved that they failed to implement safety procedures.

Fig 1.17 Workers handling food must comply with hygiene rules

Accidents that happen in the workplace are always investigated, even minor cuts and bruises should be recorded in the accident book. A record of the accident can then be checked and compared to other accidents that have happened before. If similar accidents have happened it may mean that a piece of equipment has become dangerous, or staff have been incorrectly trained.

Major accidents are often investigated by the HSE, and companies can be taken to court if they are found to be responsible for the accident.

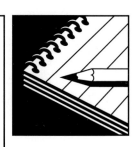
ACTIVITIES

1. List the safety rules that apply on building sites.

2. Hygiene rules safeguard the consumer and food production workers. Describe how these rules can be monitored.

3. The textile industry in the nineteenth century had a very bad safety record. Describe the risks involved in working on a modern shirt production line.

PORTFOLIO NOTES

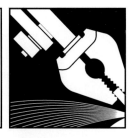

List all of the safety and hygiene issues relating to your product and show what you are doing to ensure safe working practices during production.

Quality standards

Generally speaking, the quality of manufactured goods is high. This is because a sophisticated public demands high quality products. Some products would work just as well if they were not finished to a very high standard, but would probably not sell well because they would not look attractive.

Motorcars have very high production quality controls, not only for safety but also for the finish of the bodywork and the quality of the interior.

Most clothing would work just as well if it was poorly finished, so long as it did not come apart, but we require the finish of the stitching, the buttons, the hems and so on to be of a high standard because we want it to look good.

Fig 1.18 A quality finish will cost the consumer more

Safety requirements often help raise the overall finish of a product. Think of a motor car; things like sharp edges on the body work, roughly welded metal, poor paintwork or poorly fitted engine components may affect the safety of the car, as well as how long it will last.

If the consumer demands a very high standard of finish to their products they usually have to pay more, as the production process is longer. Attention to detail will always cost more.

It is often possible to achieve a working product relatively cheaply, but to achieve a quality product often takes greater investment at every stage.

- The design needs to be carefully thought through and tested at every stage.

- The product needs to be modelled extensively and tested again.

- The proposed market needs to be researched carefully.

- The product needs to be manufactured with the best possible materials and components.

- The production process needs to be monitored carefully.

All of this costs money. Manufacturers spend a lot of money on quality control in order to maintain sales and get customer loyalty. The market the product is aimed at will usually dictate the quality and price of the product. Consumers will sometimes accept slightly poorer finishes if the product is cheaper to buy.

Some products have to be made to a very high standard or they will not fulfil their function. For example, medical goods and prescription drugs are made to extremely high quality standards. If they weren't the effect they could have on a patient may be unpredictable and this could lead to disastrous results.

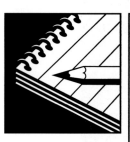

ACTIVITIES

1. Produce a report explaining when you think quality standards are more important than price.

2. Look at the quality of the next chocolate bar you buy. Is it well presented and prepared? How do you think the manufacturers maintain high standards of production?

KEY WORDS

Quality standards   the standard the product has to meet, often in safety, strength or performance

Quality control   ways of making sure the products produced meet the quality standards

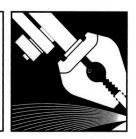

PORTFOLIO NOTES

Find out what legal standards apply to the type of product you are making. Make sure your design is able to meet these standards.

MATERIAL DETAILS AND CONSTRAINTS ④

Throughout your life you have been using different materials to make things. All materials are good at some things and bad at others. The things they are bad at puts constraints on using them. A mud hut would probably be fine in the summer in this country but would wash away in the winter because mud dissolves when it gets wet. Mud is quite strong when it is dry but not when it is wet. A constraint on using mud would therefore be that it could not be used in situations where it would get wet.

You need to know how materials perform in different circumstances so that you can choose the best ones for your design and manufacturing proposals. When comparing materials, components, and ingredients you will need to consider the following:

- are they easy to get hold of – is there a variety of suppliers to choose from?

- can you get a regular supply – do the suppliers have a regular delivery schedule?

- is the price of the material constant, or will there be times when it is more expensive?

- seasonal materials – are the materials only available at certain times of the year?

- handling problems – are the materials difficult to work, store or transport?

- what conditions will the product be used in, and

what are the best materials to stand up to those conditions?

Setting up a company to make fresh strawberry pies could lead to difficulties with supplies. Strawberries are seasonal and, out of season, are very expensive to import from abroad.

You need to consider how your materials work and perform. Does your product need to flex, be waterproof and withstand weather conditions, be stored or transported cheaply? Is the material going to be expensive or difficult to obtain?

Is your product safe for people to use, or does it need to be protected in some way? Food products need to

Fig 1.19 Importing fresh produce from abroad can be costly

be packaged to protect them from bacteria that would cause them to go bad. Medical supplies must also be kept hygienically. Storing your product may cost money. Flat packs, for instance, save money by taking up less space in a warehouse, in delivery and in the showrooms.

ACTIVITIES

1. Make a list of the materials required to construct a garden gate. Think about its environment and what it has to withstand throughout one year.

2. When packaging a box of chocolates the manufacturers have to give the designer a brief. This will include manufacturing constraints. List what they may be for this type of product.

KEY WORD

Constraints   things that might limit what can be done, such as the handling, storage, or transportation of a product

PORTFOLIO NOTES

What constraints will your materials have to work under? What makes the materials you have chosen the right ones for the job?

Material Designs and Constraints

In order to design or manufacture a product you will need to know something about materials and their properties, to ensure the product functions correctly. It doesn't matter if it is a new ice cream or a motorbike, understanding your material and its properties is vital to the success of your project. Through this understanding you should be able, as a manufacturer, to select the most appropriate materials for each component. It is at this stage you may also look at the sustainability of the material you will be using.

Manufacturers will look at the following questions.

- Where do the materials come from?

- Will they need to be transported long distances or are they easy to get hold of? The further they have to be transported the more costly they are likely to be.

- Is there likely to be a constant, reliable supply?

- Would it be more economical to get the product manufactured near the source of supply?

- Do the materials need to be stored in a specialized store? Do they need to be protected from water, heat, light or theft?

Manufacturers will need to know the advantages and disadvantages of materials in order to check their suitability for the product, for example, how do they perform in different environments?

The cost of materials is very important and sometimes they are too expensive, in which case the design will have to be modified or re-costed. Some material costs fluctuate such as those for gold, platinum or meat products.

Health and safety also need to be considered. Some materials are obviously very dangerous at certain stages in production, for example radioactive materials used in smoke alarms. Hygiene is also very important in the manufacture of foods.

Once the product has been manufactured you need to think about how well it will last if stored. In food products this is vital as food products that are not chilled may deteriorate if they are packaged incorrectly. Some foods will be destroyed if handled incorrectly or stored inappropriately.

Fig 1.20 Grain needs to be stored in specialized silos

ACTIVITIES

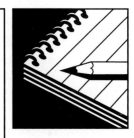

1. Some manufacturing material can be dangerous for workers. Can you think of any such materials and what precautions could be used to protect the workers?

2. Sometimes manufacturers get it wrong and choose the wrong materials. Can you think of any such products?

Record your answers to both of these activities and present them as a poster.

KEY WORDS

Properties the qualities of the material, such as how strong it is, whether it flows easily, etc.

Sustainability whether the material uses a resource from the earth that is not being replaced

Suitability how good the material will be at doing a particular job

Storage how the material needs to be kept before it is used

Cost all of the above will affect the cost of the material

PORTFOLIO NOTES

Make notes about all the materials you considered for your project, not just the ones you used.

Explain why you chose certain materials and why you rejected others.

Material Availability, Form and Supply

Manufacturers rely on a regular and consistent supply of material from their material supplier. If this chain fails then production stops and money is lost. Therefore it is important to make sure reliable supplies are available for the materials you are thinking of using.

The way in which materials are supplied can alter the cost of a product. The more work that goes into refining a material before it is used to make things, the more it will cost. For example, drawn steel wire is more expensive per kilo than cast iron. The designer must bear in mind the possible product material type, form and availability: this is all part of finding the best solution.

The form in which material is delivered to manufacturers also affects storage, transportation costs and preparation for the manufacturing purposes. Wood may come in planks, sheets or blocks; it really depends on the needs of the manufacturer. Rough wood may be cheaper to buy, but planed wood might cut down manufacturing costs. A biscuit factory may be happy to use dried raw materials but may find it quicker to produce some types of biscuits if some of the ingredients arrive premixed or partially prepared. A steel manufacturer may prepare steel in a certain form to speed up the manufacturing process of a product made by another company. This of course will add to the initial costs but may be more economical in the long run.

Fig 1.21a This metal is delivered in rolls

Fig 1.21b Wool is delivered in bales

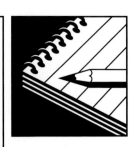

ACTIVITIES

1. Describe a manufacturing industry that is dependent on seasonal availability in order to make its products.

2. Try to work out how the industry can be flexible with what they produce to avoid problems with supply and demand.

3. Describe the factors you think add to the cost of materials.

KEY WORDS

Availability how easy it is to get the material you need

Form the shape the material comes in

Supplier where the material is bought

Storage how the material needs to be kept

PORTFOLIO NOTES

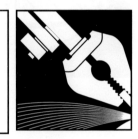

Where would you buy your material from if you had to buy it in bulk? Does any of it need special storage? Is one particular form more useful than another? Can you buy any pre-finished parts that will cut down manufacturing time, or would they be too expensive?

Material Properties, Characteristics and Performance

All materials have unique properties and characteristics. In other words they look, feel and perform differently. This means that they are more suitable for one product than they are for another. As a manufacturer you will need to choose the best material for your products. In order to do this you need to know what each material does well, what each does poorly, if they can be modified and how well they will work on the equipment you have.

Plastic is a good example of this (see Figure 1.22 overleaf), and another example is steel. It comes in many forms and some work better in some environments than others: some are stronger and some are more resistant to various forces, and so on. Steel is an alloy, which means it has other things added to it when it is being made, and these change its properties. Adding chromium, for instance, makes stainless steel, which doesn't rust like many steels do and doesn't need to be protected. It costs more than ordinary steel, though, and it is harder to work.

Different varieties of apple have different flavours, cooking times, textures and perform differently when cooked. Therefore, in order to produce sound food products you need to know which kind of apple to choose.

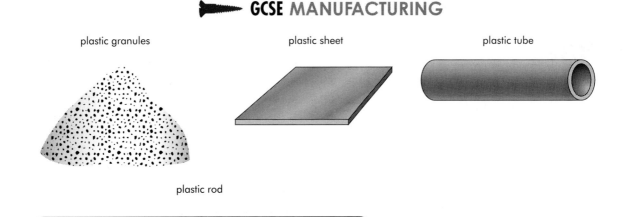

plastic granules

plastic sheet

plastic tube

plastic rod

Fig 1.22 There are thousands of different types of plastic or polymer, each designed for a specific job, and all have different characteristics. The manufacturer has to choose the right one.

ACTIVITIES

1. Choose a product you can describe in detail and suggest an inappropriate material for the product, for instance, a wooden car. Explain why this might be an inappropriate material.

2. It is important to know how materials behave when choosing which one to use for a product. Explain why this is something a designer needs to know about.

KEY WORDS

Properties the qualities that describe a material

Characteristics the things that make a material different from other materials

Performance how well a material does certain things

PORTFOLIO NOTES

List the data sources you used to find out about your materials.

Material Costs

Manufacturers are always trying to bring the cost of their products down in order to be competitive. One way they can do this is to reduce material costs. There are several ways they can try to do this:

- calculate the strength of the product carefully, so they are not using thicker material than they need to

- use a smaller range of materials so that they can buy in bulk and save money

- look for cheaper suppliers

- design the product so it uses less expensive materials

- plan the process carefully so that they can order 'just in time'. This means that the materials only arrive when they are about to be used. This means that they are not paid for as early, cash flow is improved and storage costs are reduced.

Buying at the right time is often the key to cutting costs, for instance if you were making strawberry jam in December in northern Europe, the strawberries would have to be imported, and therefore they would cost a lot more.

Sometimes higher costs are justified because the materials are environmentally friendly, but more costly to produce. This could be offset against a slightly higher selling price, which consumers may be prepared to pay if they value the environment. Organic produce is an example of this: it costs more to grow, but many people feel it is better for their health, and so will pay the higher price.

There could also be reasons such as a particular material is the only one that will do the job, or the customer wants a particular material for aesthetic reasons. Gold is the traditional material for wedding rings and not many people would want one made in stainless steel or plastic just because it was cheaper.

The factors affecting material cost are as follows:

- transportation – how far away is the source of the raw material? How heavy or bulky is it?

- processing of materials – how much refining of the raw material is needed?

- availability – is the material available throughout the production run?

- storage – how much space is needed? Does the material need special storage such as refrigeration?

- cost of production – would a cheaper material cost more to work with?

- reliability of delivery – is there likely to be a problem with getting the material when it is needed?

- time of year – is there a seasonal difference in availability?

Fig 1.23 Logs cut from a rainforest may need to be transported many miles to be processed

ACTIVITIES

1. Metal prices often fluctuate in cost per tonne or ounce. Have a look on the Internet to see which ones change most frequently over a year. Gold, silver and platinum, for example, often change daily.

2. Explain why some seemingly identical food products cost less than others.

KEY WORDS

Competitive   keeping retail prices lower than other people who are selling the same product

Buy in bulk   to buy a large quantity of material so that the price is reduced

Environmentally friendly   a material that does not use up resources, is not difficult to replace and does not cause pollution

Just in time   delivery of products exactly when you need them

PORTFOLIO NOTES

Justify the cost of the products you use. If you choose softwood rather than hardwood because it's better for the environment, then say so. You might choose to use only organic vegetables for the same reason. Include the fact that your product is environmentally friendly in your advertising material.

Health, Safety and Hygiene Requirements

Health and safety laws require that workers are safe and free from unnecessary danger when working. Along all production lines, machinery is guarded and machines have mechanisms that would stop the machines or lines if the guards were removed or incorrectly set. Manufacturing anything involves risk, whether it is cooked products or mass-produced cars. People's lives could be at risk if managers did not follow the laws that require them to act responsibly towards their workers.

Hygiene is a priority in any manufacturing plant that has anything to do with food. The materials that are used, the layout of rooms, the floors, walls and ceilings all have to reach certain standards in order to operate. These are usually checked on a regular basis.

When producing a product it may be more economic to send parts of it to specialist manufacturers who are set up for a particular process or have a production line that is geared up to work with toxic materials, rather than set these up yourself. Sometimes part of the product may be manufactured elsewhere for these reasons.

The Health and Safety at Work acts and European laws all protect the workers in manufacturing and ensure that certain hygiene standards are met. There is more information on these regulations later in this book.

Fig 1.24 Specific health and safety requirements must be met when working with toxic materials

ACTIVITIES

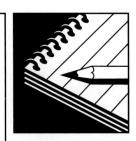

1. You will have already come across safety or hygiene laws and rules in school. Produce a report explaining why you think they are in place in some areas and not others, and what costs they add to setting up the rooms.

2. Draw a diagram of the safety features in your workroom.

KEY WORDS

Health   making sure a worker does not become ill

Safety   making sure the worker does not have an accident

Hygiene   keeping products free from bacteria that might cause illness

PORTFOLIO NOTES

What health, safety and hygiene requirements apply to your product? How would you make sure the people making the product followed them? Can you design something that will help with safety, such as a jig to hold a component securely while it is being drilled?

Materials Handling and Storage

The name given to the way materials are transported around the factory or manufacturing plant is 'materials handling'. You will probably have a number of pieces of equipment and machinery fixed to the floor in the school or college workshop and you will carry the materials to these pieces of machinery. In manufacturing companies, all sorts of devices are used to transport the materials including fork lift trucks, conveyors and robots.

There are two types of materials handling systems: fixed path systems, such as chutes, conveyors, rail cars, elevators and tubes, which cannot be changed; variable path systems that can transport to variable routes such as fork lift trucks, tractors and cranes. Generally fixed path systems are used for mass and large scale manufacture and variable path systems are used for one-off and batch manufacture. Fixed path systems are usually fully automatic.

Sometimes the power tools are taken to the materials. When you create a materials handling system, safety is of prime importance. Many transport systems have moving parts such as pulleys, belts, gears and motors.

Manufacturing costs will increase if materials need to be stored or handled in a special way. Stocks of material cost money – until materials are turned into products they are not making any money. Many large manufacturers operate what is known as JIT (just in time); they only order materials when they are about to be used. This saves on storage space and if the manufacturing lines break down they do not have vast stocks to look after.

The handling of materials is more important in some industries than others. Materials used by the food industry need to be handled carefully, or they will become stale or go bad. This may involve specialist storage that might be expensive. Food products need to be stored in cool, dry environments, some need to be refrigerated, and this adds to the overall production costs. Flammable materials will need special storage too.

Textiles also have particular storage requirements. Fabric is stored in rolls, because that is how it is manufactured. It doesn't take up much space, but when in use the fabric has to be laid out and can take up an enormous amount of space. Therefore, it is important that manufacturers try to minimize the amount of time the fabric has to be laid flat.

Handling can be a problem for materials that are very heavy, and specialized lifting equipment may be needed. Materials that break easily will require careful handling, and this may be expensive too.

Fig 1.25 Cheese needs to be stored in a cool room

Material costs increase if they need lots of handling or are to be stored for a long time. This is usually because the manufacturer will have to pay for the storage space and more workers will be needed (their wages will be added to the production costs).

When deciding on storage the following considerations ought to be taken into account:

- some materials will deteriorate if stored outside
- food products need specialist storage facilities. Cheese, for instance, requires cool rooms, which are expensive to maintain
- hazardous materials need specialist storage facilities and must be clearly labelled
- many products need clean or dust-free environments for storage
- some materials need to rest for a time before they can be used, for example cast iron.

ACTIVITIES

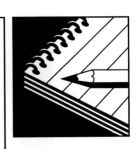

1. Investigate industries that use JIT and explain why. Do an Internet search to find out more about the JIT process.

2. List the foods you ate today. Try to find out where they came from and how they might have been stored before you ate them.

3. Explore a range of materials handling systems and state what they are used for and if they are fixed or variable systems.

4. List a range of storage considerations for your chosen materials area.

KEY WORDS

Deteriorate   become gradually worse, for instance by going rusty

Hazardous   dangerous

Handling   how a product must be treated when it is moved

Shelf life   how long a material can be stored and still be usable

PORTFOLIO NOTES

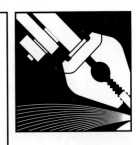

Do any of the materials you use need to be stored carefully? Food products may need refrigeration and will have a best before date on them. What is the shelf life of the materials you are using?

List any specialist materials you will be using and state how they will be stored, clearly indicating any problems associated with long-term or incorrect storage.

QUALITY STANDARDS – TOLERANCES ⬡5

Tolerance is the amount a product can vary in size, weight, colour or shape from its original specification. It is almost impossible to get everything exactly the same size, but it is possible to get them within a tolerable range so they still work.

In an engine, the tolerance between components will be extremely small, whereas in a pre-built house section, it may be within plus or minus 0.6 mm. This means that for a part that should measure 10 mm, it will pass quality checks if it is anywhere between 9.4 and 10.6 mm.

The level of tolerance set really depends on what the component does and how well it has to perform. The weight of packaged food must come within a certain tolerance so that they all weigh about the same. It is important that the food does not weigh less than is advertised on the packet, so the tolerance set might

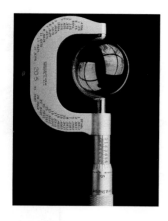

Fig 1.26 Using a micrometer to test tolerance

be 0 to 5 g. That means a 100 g package could weigh up to 105 g but must not fall below 100 g.

Tolerances are critical to almost any product, if they are to work well and to maintain standards. Simple products like jam have a certain thickness. If the jam were very runny we would say it performed poorly because jam is not expected to be runny.

There is very little tolerance for parts in a jet engine; they must be consistent and accurate. This is because the parts are exposed to tremendous forces and any failure would be disastrous.

Drug companies have to be very precise with the volume of each ingredient they put into a tablet. Active ingredients are measured in parts per billion. If the tolerances were wrong, one tablet may be stronger or weaker than the next; this would cause different results for the patient.

Very high tolerance standards in any product will cost money and the product will cost more. However, higher tolerance standards usually improve the quality of a product.

To speed up the inspection process, special gauges are often produced. Acceptable quality means that a product or component matches the tolerance standards specified in the design. Sometimes a product can be reworked, for example, a component that is too long may be able to be shortened, but at other times the product has to be scrapped, for example, a product that is too short might not be able to be lengthened. The gauges used are often referred to as 'go'–'no-go' gauges. Gauges can measure length, shape, diameter and curves. Because gauges do not need an operator to read measurements they reduce the chance of human error. Some modern gauges use laser beams to give very precise measurements.

ACTIVITIES

1. We use tolerance every day to ensure products are fit for work. The top of your pen has a very low tolerance otherwise it would not stay on. Describe five other products that you use every day that have been engineered to high tolerance standards.

2. Clothing manufacturers use standard sizes that fit a range of people in this part of the world. What are the tolerances between the sizes? Try to find out how much a size 12 is allowed to vary. It can get complicated because some items of clothing are intended to fit more tightly than other items.

3. Explore the use of 'go'–'no-go' gauges in manufacturing.

KEY WORD

Tolerance   the amount a product can vary and still be acceptable

PORTFOLIO NOTES

Make sure you set realistic tolerances for the things you make and state how you will check to ensure these tolerances are maintained.

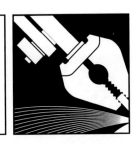

Level of Output During Production

If manufacturers are to meet production deadlines, they must make sure that output stays at the correct level. This means that the equipment and machinery has to be set up correctly and maintained properly. If this does not happen breakdowns can cause the plant to lose valuable production time. If the equipment is not set up properly, the items produced may be scrapped or need extra work, which is called rectification.

If the machine is not maintained properly, it may need to be run at a slower rate to maintain product quality. When an operator turns down the feed and speed rate of a machine in order to maintain the quality of the product, the plant produces fewer units per hour. A plant that produces eight units per hour instead of the planned ten units per hour experiences a 20 per cent reduction in manufacturing efficiency for that piece of equipment.

Once production starts, hundreds, thousands or even millions of items can be produced. Some machines

Fig 1.27 Equipment must be set up properly – to avoid costly mistakes!

run 24 hours a day, seven days a week in order to maximize production and profits.

Production lines are inspected to make sure products meet the correct standards. The amount of products that are checked depends on the type of product being produced. Some products, for instance those used in aircraft, are vitally important and every item will be checked. This is expensive, but it means that any problems are spotted quickly and actions can be carried out to try to avoid any loss of production.

ACTIVITIES

1. Investigate a range of industries that run production lines 24 hours a day, seven days a week. Explain why they have to do this.

2. Explain why continuous production methods are difficult to maintain with a small workforce.

KEY WORDS

Inspection   checking a product for faults

Rectification   correcting problems and faults

Scrap   throwing a product away because it cannot be used or rectified

PORTFOLIO NOTES

How will you check the quality of your product? What will you measure and how will you do it? How will you record the results of the tests?

Level of Performance of the Product

If a new tent was only waterproof for two days, was heavy to carry and blew down in light winds, we would say it performed badly. The function of a tent is to provide shelter, to be durable and to stand up to the conditions it was designed for. Function needs to be considered at the design stage, the designer must make sure that the specified material will be suitable for the function of the product.

In order for manufacturers to produce a satisfactory product they need to check functionality and materials, together with design ideas. All these components should come together to produce a suitable product.

Performance is an important consideration for all products that are produced. Food items, such as ready-made trifles, need to maintain their shape until the specified 'use by' date. The trifle would be performing poorly if the cream dissolved and the base

Fig 1.28 A tent should provide shelter in all weather conditions

liquefied because of a short car journey: the customer would not be happy with the product.

Some products have to perform well in the environments they were created for otherwise the result would be catastrophic. Examples of this are engine parts, aircraft components and safety devices. It is only through thorough testing that we can make sure a product will perform well over time.

This extensive testing adds to the overall quality of the product, but is expensive. This means that good quality products are more expensive to purchase than poor quality products. The cheaper products may have been produced without as much time and money being invested to test the product.

ACTIVITIES

1. Have you ever bought a product that has failed, perhaps a pen that leaked? List products that have failed you and suggest the reasons why.

2. Describe three products you would consider vital, and explain how you would survive if they failed.

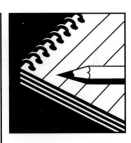

KEY WORD

Durability   how long a product will last in certain working conditions and environments

PORTFOLIO NOTES

Will it be possible to test the performance of your finished product?

If so, how will you do it?

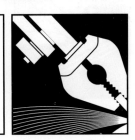

Product Finish, Packaging and Presentation

The finish of a product is very important, part of the aesthetics of the product. We like to see smooth edges, sharp corners (or beautifully rounded ones),

neat seams and accurate printing. The finish helps to attract us to buy a product.

Finish can mean many different things, it does not always mean smooth. It is the surface appearance of the product, which could be textured, ribbed, matt, gloss and so on.

Some manufactured products rely heavily on the way in which they are presented. All manufacturers know that the right packaging can help sell their products, and the wrong packaging even on a good product could cause it to fail.

Books often sell because of their cover design; chocolate boxes sometimes cost more to produce than the chocolates inside. Putting a simple product, like a computer game CD, into a big and attractive box improves its perceived value, the amount we think it is worth. When the game is released again later as a budget title, it is sold in a CD jewel case.

Fig 1.30 Some packaging designs become synonymous with the product

Fig 1.29 Chocolate boxes often cost more to produce than the chocolates themselves

Many design problems are about how to package a product. The packaging needs to perform well, not only to contain the product, but also to make the product look good.

Personal stereos made by different companies may contain the same mechanisms. However, customers are influenced by the look and feel of the packaging and will buy the one that they think looks the best.

Quality controls throughout the manufacturing process should ensure the finish is up to the specified standards.

ACTIVITIES

1. Some people would say packaging is a waste. Others would argue that on food products the packaging is vital as it contains and protects the food, keeping the product in a hygienic environment. What do you think?

2. Take a box of chocolates and try to work out how many processes are involved in the production of the pack. Describe the manufacturing processes in order.

PORTFOLIO NOTES

State how you intend to finish/package/present your product, describing why you have chosen these particular methods over others.

DEVELOPING DESIGN IDEAS ⬡6

The first step in developing a design idea is to look at the design brief, which is your base; everything else comes from this starting point.

As a manufacturer you will have to assume that the designer has followed a series of carefully considered steps to reach the final design. Ideas should be based on the following:

- the material that should be used

- how the product will be manufactured

- what standards the product has to be made to.

Fig 1.31 Most design work is now done on computer

All designers start with the same basic framework in order to achieve their goal, the final design. In order to do this they will look at similar products for sale in the shops at the moment. They must know how different materials work and how they can be made into products.

The research process usually involves working with the potential customer. The designers will then start

drawing a variety of simple ideas and rejecting the weaker ones until they have come up with one idea that best answers the brief.

Most design work is now done on computers. The designer can produce 3D models, change colours and shapes quickly and even apply textures to see what different materials and finishes would look like. The use of computers is covered in greater detail later.

Designers need to look at:

- production methods

- materials, and material properties

- how much each component may cost

- who will buy the product (the market)

- the quality of the finished product, how accurate it has to be, and what it will look like when finished.

The designer has to justify the design, including parts that may add cost but be worthwhile, and make the product work well or sell better. Each design idea should be considered against a set of design criteria:

- function – what has the product got to do?

- form – what sort of shape can it be?

- cost – how much will each unit cost?

- durability – what conditions will it have to work in? How long will it last?

- ergonomics – how big can it be?

- aesthetics – what can it look like?

- ease of manufacture – can it be made?

- standardization – can standard components be used?

A successful product will have been carefully considered against each of the criteria, before making it into production.

ACTIVITIES

1. Try a lightning design process in five minutes: give yourself a brief, produce five or six initial design sketches and refine these down to two final designs. Make a decision on the final one and explain your choice.

2. Take a product that costs less than 50p, and try to work out how it was made and who it was designed for (the market).

KEY WORDS

Design brief statement of what is required from the product

Materials, manufacture and standards requirements you need to consider from the start of the project

Research finding out more about what the customer wants

Design criteria a list of requirements that your product must meet

PORTFOLIO NOTES

Record your initial ideas and include them in your portfolio, even if they are rough at this stage. They are a record of how you spent your time and will show how your ideas developed.

Show evidence of your research, and write up details of discussions you have with the client. Make a list of the web sites you have visited to find out about such things as health and safety. Print out your computer-based work and include it in your portfolio.

Draw up a clear list of your design criteria. This list will be used later to judge whether the final product was a success or not.

Researching and Analysing Existing Products and Manufacturing Processes

Manufacturers examine products made by other companies in order to find out how they were made and what processes were used to make them. This is called product disassembly. When starting to produce a new product, researchers will report back on what

exists at the moment that may be similar: what products are being sold and what markets they are targeting.

It is always interesting for manufacturers to look at products from rivals and try to improve upon the design or to produce a cheaper alternative in order to capture the market. They must be careful not to break the law, as patents or copyright protect products, and anyone copying them could face prosecution.

The chosen manufacturing processes will affect the final production cost. This does not only apply to resistant materials such as steel or wooden products. It also applies to food and drink and the clothing industry, which relies on designers to lead them towards the new fashions each year. Every year there are fashion shows, specialist exhibitions and so on, where designers or manufacturers show off their latest products. Unfortunately for some, a number of the people looking round these shows are competitors who will be there to get ideas, or to steal designs. This can mean that the company showing their latest design actually loses out to a competitor in the market place.

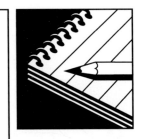

ACTIVITIES

1. Investigate a high street store that is selling clothes based on the latest designs from the top fashion designers. Describe how you can see their influence in the clothing offered for sale.

2. Disassemble something you no longer require and try to work out what processes were involved in its manufacture.

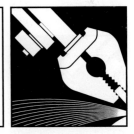

PORTFOLIO NOTES

Make sure that you include the sources of any information used in your portfolio.

Discussing Your Ideas With Others

Designers often have brainstorming or 'mind shower' sessions, where ideas that are loosely related to the design brief are discussed and explored. By doing this they can create lots of ideas very quickly and discuss them with each other, so the final concept is based on the whole group's input and not one person's ideas. Once the session is over they select all of the possible ideas and decide on one or two that may be worth investigating further. This type of teamwork will help people to share ideas and probably result in a better product design produced over a shorter period of time.

Fig 1.32 Designers will work together to brainstorm ideas

Many designers bring in potential customers (the market) and discuss ideas with them to help understand their needs and desires. This is usually done during the modelling and prototyping stage of the design, as this is when customers can see the first versions of the product in three dimensions.

Car manufacturers will bring in people their marketing departments have targeted as potential customers. They will show them mock-ups of the bodywork, interiors, colours, textures and so on, in order to get feedback. The product will then be modified as a result of these meetings. Food tasting is very common when new food products are launched.

There is a whole industry established to produce fakes, or copies of original designs, often of a much poorer quality. Manufacturers have to be careful to keep some of their ideas to themselves, or to protect them using the copyright and patent laws.

Many manufacturers will allow groups of school pupils to visit their factories, but may not allow photographs to be taken of production facilities, or particular stages in the production process. Competitors could use the photographs to find out how a certain product has been made.

ACTIVITIES

1. Discuss your design with others in order to get some feedback about your ideas.

2. Record any comments that are made, and incorporate them into your designs, showing clearly how your design developed.

PORTFOLIO NOTES

Carefully record any discussions you have and add the information to your portfolio. You can use tape, video or notes to record the discussions. Questionnaires are another useful way of gaining other people's opinions.

Freehand Sketching of Ideas

Freehand sketching is a very fast way to record and communicate ideas. It is not a new idea and has been around for centuries (see Figure 1.33 opposite), but it works; before you go to a computer, sit down, think about the design brief, and start to draw. The more ideas you can think of, the greater the chances of finding a possible outcome.

All designers sketch; some of the best designs were sketched out first on bits of paper, freehand. The Mini car, a revolution in its time because of the way the engine was mounted, and the E-type Jaguar both began life as a freehand sketch. They were then refined into a finished design and finally presented to the manufacturers for production.

A freehand sketch can also be annotated (have notes attached), as these notes can be very useful when trying to explain your thoughts to another person.

When designers sketch they do not always worry too much about the quality of their drawing, they are more interested in visualizing ideas. However, even the roughest sketches need to be legible otherwise it will be difficult to see what you were trying to convey.

However, a good freehand sketch has a quality of its own, which when done well can be used as part of a presentation. When drawing freehand, do just that; do not worry about using a ruler or a rubber at this stage, mistakes do not matter, just move on to the next space.

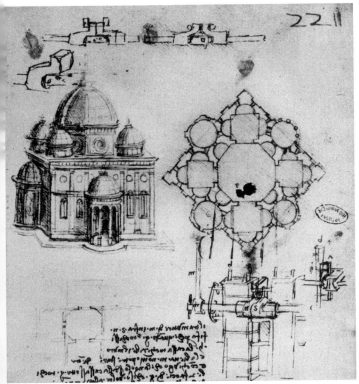

Fig 1.33 Leonardo Da Vinci used freehand sketches in the fifteenth century

ACTIVITIES

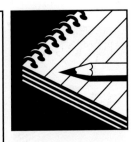

1. Try to produce a page of ten freehand sketches in four minutes, based on one of your design ideas.

2. Sketch a friend's clothes, showing shape and form, with no great detail. Do not worry about any slight mistakes. If you go wrong, start again on the same bit of paper.

PORTFOLIO NOTES

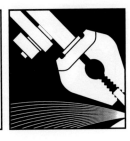

Freehand sketching is an essential way of recording your ideas. Do not throw away rough sketches as these can help you gain marks in your portfolio.

Modelling and Testing Ideas

Product modelling has undergone enormous changes over the last ten years due to the arrival of reasonably-priced computer modelling packages. These packages can give a three-dimensional image of a design or component, which can be quickly modified on the screen. However, not everyone has access to this software or the time to learn how to use it.

A scale model is an excellent way of moving your idea from paper to a tangible product that you can walk around and hold. Presenting a model to potential customers or manufacturers is not new. It is a very effective way of presenting ideas. Alterations can be easily made and will be relatively inexpensive at this stage.

If you test people's reactions to your models you will be able to judge if your design fulfils the product specification and original brief.

Highly skilled technicians make the product models. The first model is called a 'mock-up'. Mock-ups are usually made from easily worked materials, such as card, foam board, clay, polystyrene or balsa wood. They enable the technician to make the model quickly and easily, but still show how the product should appear once it is produced. Designers and manufacturers use models so that they can find where potential problems may arise that were not evident from the initial drawings. The mock-up is often a scale

Fig 1.34 An example of an architectural model

model of the product, so a number of physical tests can also be carried out. Tests that would be too costly to leave until the product has been manufactured, strength tests, for example, can be carried out on the model.

ACTIVITIES

1. Some food products are modelled for shape and form. Describe why this would be useful.

2. Produce a simple model of your ideas before production and ask people what they think, not about the model but about the ideas you are trying to convey.

PORTFOLIO NOTES

List the methods you are going to use to model and test your own work.

Developing and Testing Samples and Prototypes

Once a model has been made and tested, manufacturers often make a sample or prototype. This is a full size, fully-functioning model. Prototypes save money because they are one-offs that can be modified by designers or model makers according to the reaction they receive from potential customers. Changes can then be made to the final product design.

Once product prototypes have been tested and refined, specialists will provide input.

- The costs of developing and applying quality control and systems must be assessed.

- Engineers will examine the manufacturing potential of the product.

- The time and money required to manufacture the product must be determined.

The final part of the process is an assessment of the financial feasibility of the new product. The skills of economists and financial experts are required for this part of the process. The goal is to work out how much money will be needed to launch a product, and to

Fig 1.35 Producing a prototype is crucial

estimate the amount of money that could be made from the sales of that product.

This is a crucial stage in the design of the product. If the prototype does all that it is supposed to do, the product will probably go into production. However, if it does not live up to expectations, even at this stage the product may be dropped. Thousands of products get to prototyping every year, but do not reach production, because of problems that are discovered at the prototype stage.

ACTIVITIES

1. Explain why a company would be foolish if they failed to produce prototypes before full-scale production.

2. Describe the information a model maker may need in order to produce a prototype model.

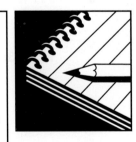

Scientific Principles

Science gives us rules and explanations about how things behave. Scientific understanding provides a foundation for all design and engineering. It would be impossible to design anything without considering some scientific ideas.

In any design work you must firstly identify what the relevant laws and rules are and then make appropriate calculations. You will need this information to include in your design.

By applying the correct scientific ideas you will be able to answer the type of questions listed overleaf.

- How strong does it need to be?

- How hot will it get?

- Will it melt at the temperatures it will be working at?

- What is the maximum load it can take?

- Will it work underwater?

- Will it break or bend if I overload it?

- How fast will it go?

- What current will the motor need?

Some of these scientific principles are easy to understand, but some are more complicated. You may also find that there are data books that will help you, which provide information about particular materials or components. There are various tests that you can carry out to ensure that the design will work, either theoretically on paper, or practically as the product is manufactured. These include:

1. Strength checks – materials and structures can be checked at the design stage using force diagrams and appropriate calculations.

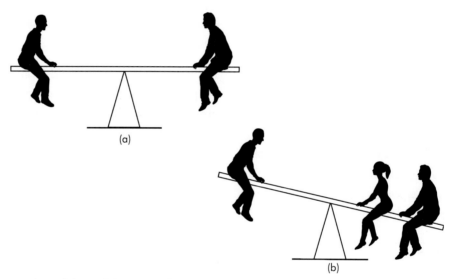

Fig 1.36 Balance is achieved by weight and distance from the pivot

The principle of movements can be used to work out when something is stable:

$$\text{Movement} = \text{Force} \times \text{Distance from pivot}$$

For the system to be stable and not to turn, it needs to be in equilibrium, so that clockwise movement equals anticlockwise movement.

2. Resultant forces – vector diagrams can be used to work out the overall effect of forces from different directions.

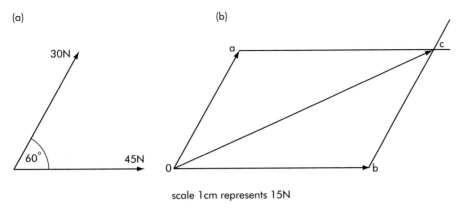

(a)

30N

60°

45N

(b)

a

c

0

b

scale 1cm represents 15N

Fig 1.37 Vector diagram

3. Beam reactions – these work out how much a support beam will bend or deflect.

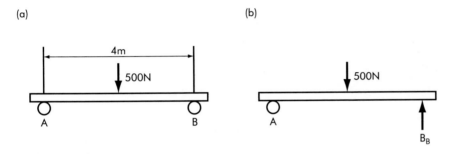

(a)

4m

500N

A

B

(b)

500N

A

B_B

Fig 1.38 Forces and supports

Materials need to be checked to make sure they can stand the forces they will be subjected to:

*   tension – being pulled
*   compression – being squashed
*   torsion – being twisted
*   shear – being ripped.

Joints also need to be tested – some joints make materials stronger, others can cause weaknesses. Test rigs can be used to test samples of the material.

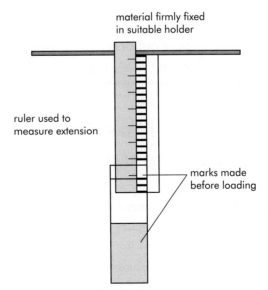

material firmly fixed in suitable holder

ruler used to measure extension

marks made before loading

Fig 1.39 To test how a material behaves under tension

ACTIVITIES

1. For one of the tests mentioned previously, design a suitable test rig.

2. Describe why testing is so important to the success of a design.

KEY WORDS

Scientific principles   the theoretical rules that help us to calculate how a product will perform

Strength checks   checks that use calculations to work out if a design is strong enough for its purpose

Strength tests   practical tests to see how strong a material is

Data books   books that list different material properties, such as the strength and density of a material

Forces   the load the product will be subjected to, such as tension, compression, shear and torsion

Joints   the way the pieces of the product are fixed together – these can be weak points in the structure

PORTFOLIO NOTES

Decide what tests you will need to carry out at each stage of your production. What scientific principles will help you work out how thick your materials need to be?

Will you carry out practical tests, such as cooking various apples to see how their texture changes? If so, explain how you will do it.

Production – Most Suitable Processes

The production manager and production engineers make decisions about which manufacturing process will be most suitable. There are lots of factors that need to be considered, such as the purpose and size of the product, the material being used and the number of products that need to be produced.

Setting up for a mass production run of two or three million products is very expensive and the manufacturers will be looking for the quickest and cheapest method. Plastics, woods, metal, food and fabric all require quite different production systems and within each material type there are literally thousands of methods of production.

It is important that processes are carried out in an efficient and appropriate order. It is no good painting a sheet of plywood, and then cutting it into sections to be fitted together into a door.

Fig 1.40 A bottling plant will have its own specific production system

The production process is broken down into different stages, using an operation process chart (see Figure 1.41 overleaf). Each part of an operation is looked at in detail, to work out the most efficient method of production. A flow process chart will be developed to identify the sub-processes that need to be carried out.

The layout of the factory also needs to be considered; with older factories this may not be possible, as the machinery cannot always be moved. Modern factory systems are usually more flexible about where machines and equipment can be positioned. There are a number of different factory layouts common in manufacturing companies.

Product layout refers to a manufacturing company where the machines are positioned so that there is a flow from raw materials to finished products. The system was designed by Henry Ford, and he used conveyor belts and long, continuous transportation systems to transport the product around the factory.

In process layouts, machines and tools are grouped together to provide areas within the manufacturing plant where certain processes take place. Products are usually moved around the factory in batches. This type of plant layout is often used for batch manufacturing.

Some products, such as ships, planes or trains sometimes have the factory built around them, so that the product does not move, but the manufacturing equipment does.

The process of manufacturing the product can begin once the production line has been set up with specialized equipment, and all the staff have been trained to use the equipment.

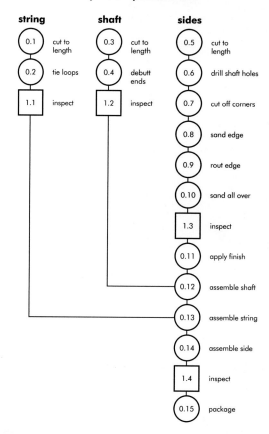

operation process chart

string
- 0.1 cut to length
- 0.2 tie loops
- 1.1 inspect

shaft
- 0.3 cut to length
- 0.4 debutt ends
- 1.2 inspect

sides
- 0.5 cut to length
- 0.6 drill shaft holes
- 0.7 cut off corners
- 0.8 sand edge
- 0.9 rout edge
- 0.10 sand all over
- 1.3 inspect
- 0.11 apply finish
- 0.12 assemble shaft
- 0.13 assemble string
- 0.14 assemble side
- 1.4 inspect
- 0.15 package

Fig 1.41 An operation process chart

ACTIVITIES

1. Suggest a suitable production method for a plastic sieve. Explain why you have chosen that method.

2. Produce an operation process chart and a flow process chart for a product you have made or will be making.

3. Draw a plant layout for your laboratory/workshop and explore ways in which it could be redesigned to improve productivity.

PORTFOLIO NOTES

When producing your portfolio, make sure you comment on the most efficient plan layout and production methods for your chosen product.

Add a plan of manufacture, identifying all of the key stages of producing your chosen product.

Materials, Size, Properties and Characteristics

Each material has properties and characteristics that are unique. Wood for instance can be turned, moulded, laminated, veneered, steamed and bent. Glass can be blown, cast, drawn, moulded, welded and tinted.

Each material is unique and the manufacturer, designer, and production engineers all need to be aware of this.

Large materials such as trees must be specially prepared for production; smaller items such as peas require specialised containers and hoppers. Most materials can be used for large production runs. It is designers and engineers who decide the most suitable or economical process for a particular product that is being designed.

The word plastic does not mean one material. Plastics come in thousands of different forms, all suitable for different products and production systems. Many plastic products are vacuum-moulded, injection-moulded or slush-moulded. The choice of process depends on the shape, size and function of the product.

Considerations for manufacturing processes are:

- the physical size of the product itself
- the number of products to be made in each run
- what the product is designed to do (its function)
- the characteristics of the product: fragile, toxic, soft, ductile, hard, small, large, and so on.

Some materials are only available from suppliers in fixed sizes; for instance, steel rod is only available in certain diameters. This is because the mills used to make the rod are very expensive, so to keep costs down the suppliers only produce certain sizes. It is left

Fig 1.42 Glass can be blown due to its unique qualities

up to the manufacturer to reform the steel if the fixed size is not appropriate. Fixings are also made to particular sizes. It is important to consider this at the design stage of production. Electrical resistors and

other components are only available in certain values. Again it is the responsibility of the designer and manufacturer to make sure that they have taken this into account before starting to make the product.

ACTIVITIES

1. Produce a report explaining how many products around you are mass-produced. Are they batch-produced or one-offs?

2. Make a list of material sizes available to you from your local supplier.

3. Make a list of the standard fixing sizes that you can use for the products you design and make.

PORTFOLIO NOTES

Make sure you record in your portfolio the reasons why you would choose certain materials and fixings over others.

Costs of Material, Resources and the Production Process

Before manufacturing starts, materials are sourced by seeking quotes from material producers. The materials could come from anywhere in the world and need to be ordered on time at the best possible prices, and be in a correct form for the production run.

The supplier also has to guarantee they will deliver the material by a certain date, so that production is not held up. Sometimes companies will fine a supplier for late delivery, and the supplier may insist on a similar clause for late payment.

The factors that determine material cost are:

- availability (seasonal products are cheaper in season)

- if the material has already been processed or partly formed

- if the material is a commodity the price will rise and fall

- the distance the material will have to be transported

- the amount of the material you need (the more you buy the cheaper it becomes)

- demand – high demand can increase the price.

Factors that may add to the cost of production are:

- the complexity of the production run

- whether specialized finishing or machining is required

- if any hand finishing is required

- the number of processes the product has to go through

- the cleaning and setting up times
- maintenance and checking during production (tension on sewing devices, etc.)
- how hazardous the production run will be
- maintaining health and safety regulations.

Fig 1.43 Buying materials in bulk can be a cheaper alternative

ACTIVITIES

1. To make jam you would need the correct materials. Imagine you are making 100,000 jars of strawberry jam. In what sequence would you order the material for the jam and what preparations would you make before production?

2. Look at your bag and try to identify how it is made. Would one producer make all the parts, or would some have to be ordered ready made?

Market Type and Size

Markets are groups of people with different lifestyles or incomes. Each group will buy different food, clothing, homes, cars and so on. For example, a professional football player in a good team might be able to buy expensive cars, and will have time and money to buy expensive holidays. A painter and decorator might be able to buy a new van or ladder and his lifestyle (how he lives) would be different to that of the wealthier football player.

Some markets are much larger than others. The market for crisps, for example, runs into billions of pounds each year and the market for handmade shoes is tiny in comparison. Nevertheless there are still companies doing very well out of small markets: usually the end product is more expensive and will have a better finish.

Most markets are based on:

- age
- income
- lifestyle
- profession.

Marketing people use these criteria to group the public into units, representing each unit by a letter and a number. A person categorized as a C2 might be a plumber and an A1 might be a barrister.

A manufacturer has to be sure that they are producing products for the right market. Carefully targeted advertising can help this.

ACTIVITIES

1. Describe the market you think a particular high street store is targeting and explain why you think this is the case.

2. Select three clothing stores and try to identify which markets they are aiming at.

PORTFOLIO NOTES

Examine existing products and their intended markets. State how your own product fits into its intended market.

7 PRESENTING DESIGN SOLUTIONS

The presentation of your design solution is as important as the solution itself. If your design is presented well, it will be clear that you have worked from the brief and developed the final design as the result of careful consideration. A slick, well-presented design idea is more likely to be understood and accepted by clients than a poorly-drawn, shoddy design.

When presenting a final design you should explain why it is the best solution. You need to justify why you chose the materials and how the design will meet the required quality standards. Clients often ask if the final design idea has been shown to potential customers and what their reactions were. Designers will usually show their final ideas by using ICT either through digital photos, 3D computer-generated images, rendered sketches on boards, production type drawings, or through models that allow the customer to handle the solution.

Computer presentations through the use of multimedia presentation packages are also very popular. Clothes and fashion designs will be shown on models, dummies or on computer-generated renderings. When making the presentation, the designer explains what aspects of the solution are most important; for example, the reason a particular colour or surface finish has been used.

Fig 1.44 Presenting your ideas is important

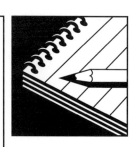

ACTIVITIES

1. Find a product that interests you and pretend you are presenting it as a model to your clients. Explain why you have decided on the materials, colours, textures and manufacturing process.

2. Can you find a product that has, in your opinion, failed to fulfil its functions? Make a list of reasons why you think it has failed. Major manufacturers still make very costly mistakes.

KEY WORDS

Presentation   the way you show your ideas

Presentation drawings   photos, computer images (2D and 3D), rendered sketches, and production drawings

Models   a 3D representation of your idea

Presentation software   an electronic slideshow

Clients   the people who are ordering the product from you

Customers   the people who will buy the product in the shops

PORTFOLIO NOTES

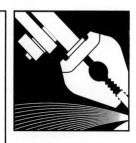

Present your work using a wide range of media. Use a variety of drawing methods to show different aspects of your design. If you produce a computerised slideshow, you can usually print it as handouts with small images of each slide, perhaps six to a page.

Remember to use the most appropriate presentation method for each stage of your work.

Presenting Your Design Solution

Key Features of the Solution, Production and Material Constraints

The design and development process should lead you to your final product solution and you should be able

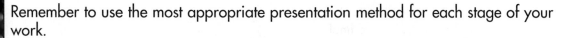

to answer a number of important questions.

- What material would be best suited for the job?
- How will the product be made (what manufacturing process or processes will produce what you need)?
- How many items will be made?

Some products are made from one part, such as a washing up bowl; some items will be made from several parts all manufactured in different ways and then assembled, for instance, a mobile phone (see Figure 1.45 below).

The function of the product will usually determine the material it is made from. For instance, if the product is to be waterproof, plastic or glass may be appropriate; if it is a casing for an external lamp, plastic or cast metal may be appropriate.

> A paper boat is easy to make, looks pretty, but will always sink
>
> *Japanese proverbs 1277*

The final design should fulfil all the specifications and address the client's brief accurately. When creating a design you should always have in mind the function and properties of the materials that could be used for the final product.

Before starting production you must be able to answer questions about the design and manufacturing process, and be able to justify all of your answers.

These questions include:

- what production methods will you use to make your product?

- what materials will you use to make your product?

- how much will each component/unit cost?

- who will buy the product (the market)?

- the quality of the finished product: how accurate must it be? what will it look like when finished?

- what has the product got to do (function)?

- what sort of shape will it be (form)?

- what conditions will it have to work in? How long will it last (durability)?

- how big can it be (ergonomics)?

To do this you must have recorded your decisions and any modifications or adaptations you have made.

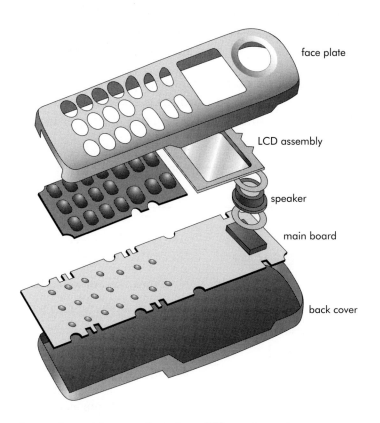

Fig 1.45 A mobile phone is made up of many different parts

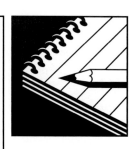

ACTIVITIES

1. Produce a checklist to show the materials and processes you have decided to use to fulfil the function and design brief for your product.

2. Produce a report justifying the decisions you have made for a product you are designing.

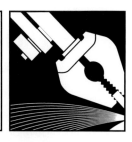

PORTFOLIO NOTES

Write a report to justify the decisions you take throughout the design and make process.

Research

Research is the keystone of any manufacturing project and is often carried out before the design brief is written, to see if there is a market for the product. Market research will reveal if people want your product. Product research will reveal what products, if any, exist at the moment as competition. Research into possible manufacturing processes, material and cost may also be carried out.

Your research could be based on the following:

- similar available products
- the prices charged for existing products
- the range of possible colours, shapes, forms and textures
- ergonomics and anthropometrics
- possible packaging solutions
- safety features or laws that are relevant to your product
- how your final product could be sold
- the environment that your product will be used in.

There are two basic types of research:

- pure research – looking for new information, without considering practical issues for the information

Fig 1.46 Market research means talking to potential customers

- applied research – looking for practical applications for the information.

Many manufacturing companies carry out pure research into things like environmental issues. Having found that a particular fuel is more efficient or a particular material is easier and cheaper to recycle, this information is then passed to the applied research team, who try to incorporate it into new design ideas.

As a designer or manufacturer you may be involved in both types of research. All your research should be annotated to explain where it came from, what use it has been and how it has influenced your design work.

ACTIVITIES

1. Look at similar products on sale at comparable prices and decide which you prefer and why.

2. List the safety features you think a chair or stool requires (check the British Standards web site, http://bsonline.techindex.co.uk, to see if you got it right).

Photographs and ICT-Generated Images

Photographic and digital images produced via a computer are used extensively in modern design and development. The main advantages of computer-derived images are that they are instant and can be sent to any part of the world quickly.

Digital cameras can help you record the progress of your products, and images can be modified in image editing software thus saving you time. Colour or shape can be changed very quickly.

Research sheets can be illustrated with digital photos, clip art or copyright-free images from the Internet.

Photographs produced using film will probably give you the best quality images and are still the basis for many computer-generated and printed images. The quality of digital photos is constantly improving and they are therefore being used more and more.

You can use images to:

• show existing products

• show different colour or shape possibilities for a product

• add illustrations to research sheets

• provide real backgrounds for a product image

• create mood boards (a set of images that have to do with the market's lifestyle or environment).

When designers present their work to the manufacturing team, or potential customers, they often use multimedia presentation software. This can incorporate still and moving images, as well as text and sound, to create a professional presentation.

However good the presentation is, the product still has to be good too. Many companies try to present products in a way that hides their faults. Photographs and digital imagery can be a great way of hiding things. Many product packages have pictures on them of what the product should look like, but often when the package is opened there are a number of differences. If a company tries to misinform the public in this way and someone complains, there may be grounds for compensation, or the company may be taken to court for misrepresenting their products.

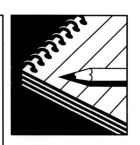

ACTIVITIES

1. When designing products, you will need to create a mood board. It must show you understand where, what and who the final design is aimed at. Designers use these all the time.

2. Produce a multimedia presentation for a product you have designed or studied. Present it to others in your group.

3. Look at design companies on the Internet and see how they present their designs. What techniques do they use?

PORTFOLIO NOTES

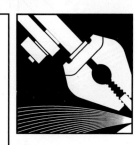

Create a mood board and include it in your portfolio.

If you use multimedia presentations, you will need to put a paper copy into your portfolio. Most presentation software lets you print out small versions to use as handouts, and these would be more suitable than big colour printouts.

Use computer techniques creatively. As well as using digital photographs to record a picture of your apple pie, you could paste it on to a background of apples.

Experiment with images of your design on computer: it is easier than changing things in real life. See how it might look in a different colour or even a different material.

Samples and Swatches

Samples and swatches of materials are used to help select the right material for a product. Designers use swatches to help them design products and production managers use them when deciding on the production processes. Costs can be worked out from them, and market research teams can show the samples and swatches to potential customers.

Material manufacturers are always willing to send samples in the hope that they will be chosen for production. It is an excellent way of seeing textures, testing durability, seeking preferences, feeling and holding the materials that the final products may be made from.

Without samples or swatches, it would only be when the product was manufactured that you would get direct contact with the materials. A garment manufacturer might produce a garment in several sample fabrics before deciding which one is easiest to sew, needs least finishing, looks better, etc. These are called prototypes. Swatches are usually for colour,

texture, fabrics, plastic or coatings. Samples are more likely to be of food or resistant materials.

When a customer decides to purchase a new car, the sales assistant may show them a range of different paint options on a swatch board. These swatches are made from small sections of material; usually the same as the body part it is meant to resemble. However, the colour shown on a small panel a few centimetres across can be very different to a whole car delivered in that colour. Similar problems may occur with food products: a small sample of a particular food item may taste great, but when you are faced with a whole plateful, it may not be quite so appealing. So although samples and swatches are useful, it is often necessary to see a large version of the material or finish. This is again where the prototype becomes so important.

Fig 1.47 Samples are useful when assessing texture and durability

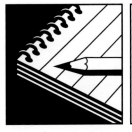

ACTIVITY

Consider a design brief you have been set, and think if swatches or samples will help in deciding a design direction. If so, contact suppliers and ask for some.

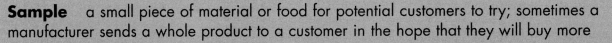

KEY WORDS

Sample a small piece of material or food for potential customers to try; sometimes a manufacturer sends a whole product to a customer in the hope that they will buy more

Swatch a small pieces of paper or fabric to help potential customers judge colours and textures

PORTFOLIO NOTES

Create your own bank of swatches, which can be added to your research work.

Presenting a Design Solution

When you decide on a final solution to a design brief you have not reached the end of the process. You must then present your ideas to the client. This is likely to consist of lots of different pieces of paper so it is important to keep everything together in a design portfolio.

Your final presentation may include:

- the initial design problem and/or client brief

- the research you carried out and the conclusions you have drawn from it

- information about the ideas process, including other possible solutions and why they were rejected

- any changes that were made during the process and why they were made

- a clear and well-presented final design solution, in a number of different formats.

You need to show that you have constantly evaluated your decisions in order to justify your final design solution. The design is your own work, made up of your choices, but you need to make sure you explain your decisions.

The presentation of your design ideas should always be as professional as you can make it. Use ICT where possible, have borders on your work and make sure each page has a title. You should also present your rough work. Sketches, rough ideas and so on are essential to explain how your design solution has developed.

Manufacturers are just like customers: they can be convinced something is a good idea if it is well presented. A poorly-presented solution will be easier to disregard. The manufacturer may think that if the presentation has not been thought through, then the ideas may not have been thought through.

However, a poor solution will usually still fail, as you will see in the next chapter. There is a lot more work to do after developing the solution before your idea becomes a well-manufactured and successful product.

PORTFOLIO NOTES

Produce a clear contents page for your portfolio, indicating what is on each page, and make sure the pages are in a logical order.

Every page should include a page number, date, your name, centre number and candidate number.

Do not put your sheets inside plastic wallets: they just add to the bulk.

Do not put in unnecessary 'padding', such as research material that you have not really analysed. The moderator is going to mark your project, not weigh it!

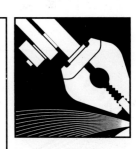

Technical Drawing and Diagrams

Once the design is complete, it is important to be able to give other people instructions about the size and shape of the design. Technical or production drawings provide clear and precise information about your design. These drawings enable manufacturers anywhere to construct a model or mock-up of the product exactly as you have drawn it.

The drawing should show the dimensions of the product so that they can be read from any angle. These drawings carry formal information that should conform to standards.

Some formal drawing systems are understood worldwide due to international standards. These types of drawing can be read and used to manufacture the product. Formal drawing systems include:

- orthographic
- planometric
- isometric
- oblique projection
- perspective.

The drawings communicate:

- shape
- form
- detail
- dimensions.

Diagrams show customers and manufacturers how things fit together and what the product should look like. Diagrams are intended to communicate your thoughts to others.

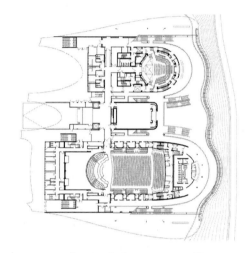

Fig 1.48 A technical diagram will convey exact size and shape

ACTIVITIES

Select a product you could work with over the next few exercises.

1. Produce a freehand sketch of the product.

2. Add colour and shading to make it look realistic.

Perspective Drawing

Perspective drawing will give you a good idea of what an object will look like, but it will not provide specific information that can be used in the design and manufacture of the object.

In perspective drawing, all lines moving away from the viewpoint converge or meet at vanishing points. These can be in the foreground or background unless the object is sloping. There can be more than one vanishing point but they must be on the same line. This line is called the horizon line.

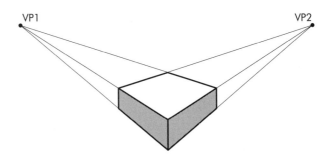

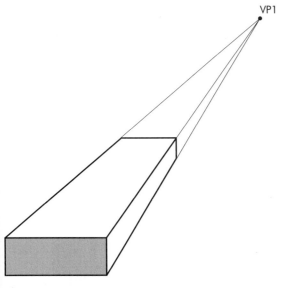

Fig 1.50 Two point perspective

Fig 1.49 One point perspective

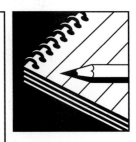

ACTIVITIES

Using the object you drew for the freehand sketch activity, draw it again but this time as:

1. A perspective drawing with one vanishing point.

2. A perspective drawing with two vanishing points.

KEY WORDS

Vanishing point   the point at which perspective lines meet

Horizon   the line where earth and sky seem to meet

Orthographic Projection

Orthographic projection is a formal technical drawing technique, which usually shows an object from three views, drawn to scale and at 90° to each other. The three views that form orthographic drawings are:

* plan

* end elevation (or view)

* side elevation (or view).

There are two ways of drawing an orthographic projection:

* first angle or English

* third angle or American.

The only difference between the two is the way the final drawing is set out. If you are able to draw one version then you can draw both.

Orthographic drawing layouts are covered by British Standards that give guidelines and symbols. These are covered in BS308, PD7308 and PP7308.

Orthographic drawings do not provide a three-dimensional representation of the product. However, they still need to be precise to give an accurate two-dimensional representation of the product or component.

Orthographic drawings often have a parts list or a material list showing which piece of material is used to make each part. Dimensions and other important features are identified on each elevation. Different types of line are used for different purposes in this method of drawing, for example a dotted line indicates hidden detail and a chain-dotted line represents the centre line. It is important to stick to these conventions.

THIRD ANGLE ORTHOGRAPHIC PROJECTION

This is the most commonly used projection. The drawing has three elevations:

- plan elevation
- side elevation under plan elevation
- end elevation to left of side elevation.

The easiest way to understand how this works is to look at this example:

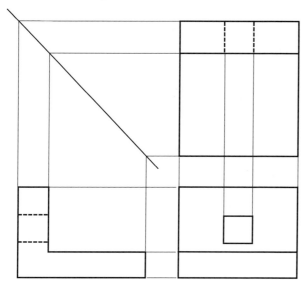

Fig 1.51 Third angle projection

HOW TO DRAW A THIRD ANGLE ORTHOGRAPHIC PROJECTION

1. Plan: Look directly down on to the top of the component and draw what you see.

2. Side elevation: Look directly at the side of the component and draw what you see.

3. End elevation: Look directly at the front of the component and draw what you see.

Constructions lines can be drawn to help you, as are shown in Figure 1.51.

HOW TO DRAW A FIRST ANGLE ORTHOGRAPHIC PROJECTION

The way to draw a first angle projection is the same but the layout is slightly different.

1. Side elevation.

2. Plan elevation under side elevation.

3. Front elevation to right of side elevation.

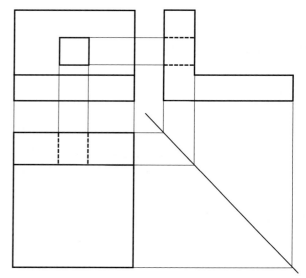

Fig 1.52 First angle projection

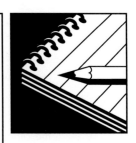
USEFUL RULES AND CONVENTIONS FOR ORTHOGRAPHIC DRAWINGS

- Dimensions are always in millimetres.

- Dimensions are written above the dimension line.

- Vertical dimensions need to be read when the drawing is turned on its side, so they must be placed on the left-hand side of the vertical dimension lines.

- The projection lines should not touch the object.

ACTIVITIES

Using the object you drew in the freehand sketch and perspective drawing exercise, draw the object again as:

1. A third angle orthographic projection.

2. A first angle orthographic projection.

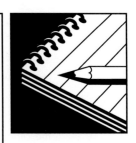

PORTFOLIO NOTES

Remember to use a range of appropriate drawing techniques throughout your portfolio.

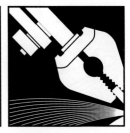

Pictorial Views

There are two pictorial views that combine sketching, perspective drawing and the information contained in orthographic projections. In both cases, true measurements can be taken from the diagrams, which are called isometric and oblique projections. They may look similar but there are some important differences.

ISOMETRIC PROJECTION

An isometric diagram is drawn with the aid of two isometric axes. These are simply two lines that start at a point in front of the object and rise up at 30° to the horizontal. Isometric paper has the isometric grid printed on it.

Rules for isometric drawing are as follows:

- all horizontal lines are at a 30° angle to the horizontal

- all vertical lines must remain vertical

- all measurements are either true or to scale.

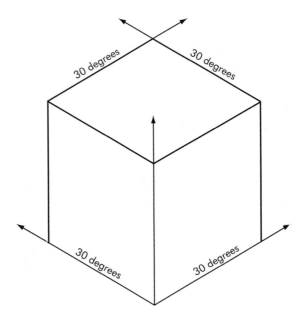

Fig 1.53 An isometric diagram

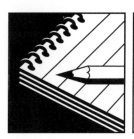

ACTIVITY

Draw the object you drew in the previous sections again but this time as an isometric projection.

OBLIQUE PROJECTION

Oblique drawing is another type of drawing technique. You begin by drawing to scale a true view of the most difficult or complicated side. You then take a line at 45° to the horizontal and use this to create the other views.

All measurements on the first face are drawn to scale. The other measurements are at half-scale (shorter). Remember that some of the dimensions are half-scale otherwise you may end up with a half-size final product.

ACTIVITY

Draw the object you drew in the previous sections again but this time as an oblique projection.

Assembly and Exploded Diagrams

Assembly and exploded diagrams are very similar and many people consider them to be the same thing. Their job is to show all the component parts of an object and how they fit together.

An assembly diagram shows how to put something together (a sequence). The most common example is flat pack furniture. Inside the packet you will get a single diagram, or series of diagrams showing you how to assemble a piece of furniture from the component parts, including the fixings needed.

The exploded view is usually a single diagram that shows all the components of an object and how they fit together. They are generally used for maintenance purposes.

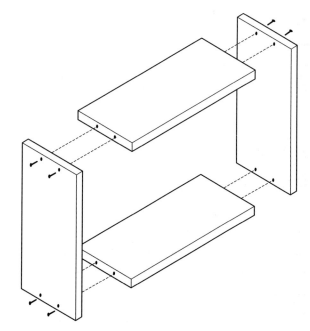

Fig 1.54 An assembly diagram

Rear hub breakdown

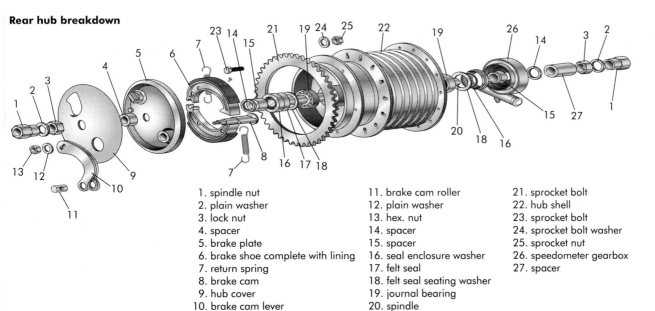

1. spindle nut
2. plain washer
3. lock nut
4. spacer
5. brake plate
6. brake shoe complete with lining
7. return spring
8. brake cam
9. hub cover
10. brake cam lever

11. brake cam roller
12. plain washer
13. hex. nut
14. spacer
15. spacer
16. seal enclosure washer
17. felt seal
18. felt seal seating washer
19. journal bearing
20. spindle

21. sprocket bolt
22. hub shell
23. sprocket bolt
24. sprocket bolt washer
25. sprocket nut
26. speedometer gearbox
27. spacer

Fig 1.55 Exploded view of a rear hub with parts list

ACTIVITY

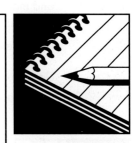

Choose one or more of the products below and draw an exploded view of it.

- Ballpoint pen
- Pencil sharpener
- CD case

PORTFOLIO NOTES

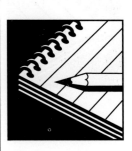

Think carefully about the types of drawings you use in your portfolio. The two main reasons for using them are to show what the finished product looks like and how to make it.

Drawings that are to be used in the manufacturing process need to stick closely to the rules that have been explained. Presentation drawings can be much more imaginative.

Try to use a variety of drawing styles to show off your range of skills. Include technical drawings that show how your product will be made. These could be done by hand or on a CAD package on computer.

Drawings should include the dimensions of the object. Choose a sensible scale for bigger objects. Include a parts list if it is appropriate to do so.

If your product is complicated to assemble, an exploded view might make it clearer.

8 MODIFYING DESIGN SOLUTIONS

Any design that has reached the market place has inevitably undergone modification, probably through the processes of testing and evaluating. Most new products are subjected to testing with customer groups (a selection of people who may buy this type of product). Any changes that need to be made to the product can then be done before it goes into full production, and the manufacturer can be sure the finished product is of the correct standard. This will save money for the manufacturer, as they will not have to make changes later.

Modifications are usually the result of testing. Once tested, the manufacturers need to look at the feedback and make any modifications. Even though the designers have followed the brief, there may still be weaknesses in the design and testing will show these up.

Good examples of the testing and product modification process are cars. Cars undergo rigorous testing over different terrains, climates and speeds, before mass production takes place. Even then it is not unusual for this process to continue during production, as completed cars are recalled to correct problems that were missed.

Testing can take many forms, depending on the nature of the product. Automated machines are used to test furniture by repeatedly dropping a weight as if someone is sitting down. Taste tests are set up for food; these often take place in supermarkets, where customers are asked to taste a sample of a new product and are then asked their opinions. The ergonomics of a product may be important. They affect how suitable the product is for the person who is using it. Handling will also test the ergonomics of the product. Most of these tests will result in some kind of modification to the design.

ACTIVITIES

1. Think of any manufactured product that you feel could do with further modifications. List them and suggest the modifications you would put in place.

2. People like to modify some of the products they buy even if they are basically OK. Think of a product you use that you have modified in some way and explain why you modified it.

KEY WORDS

Test   show the designs to people who can make useful comments about them

Evaluate   look at the results of the test and decide if any changes need to be made to the product design

Modify   make changes as a result of the tests and evaluation

Ergonomics   designing equipment to suit people, so they can use the product comfortably

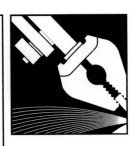

PORTFOLIO NOTES

You are likely to make modifications to your product as you develop it. Each time you do so, you should record what you changed and why you changed it. Photographs may be a quick way of recording modifications.

If you change your drawings, you should give them a new issue number so that you always know which is the latest one.

2 Manufactured Products

CHAPTER AIMS & INTRODUCTION

This chapter will explore:

- production plans and production methods
- quality control
- tools, equipment and machines
- teamwork
- materials, components and ingredients
- how to work safely
- risk assessment.

This chapter is the one that helps you get down to the part of this course you probably chose it for – making things. It helps you plan that process carefully, so that your work gets finished on time, to the correct standard and without anyone getting hurt.

All production processes are different and present different problems, but the types of problem are similar in all industries. If an operator gets long hair caught in a machine it does not matter whether that machine is for mixing dough or for cutting metal, they are still going to get hurt, and so the safety considerations are not really all that different.

Choosing the right tools, machines and processes will improve the chances of a successful product being produced safely. Of course, that does not mean that nothing can go wrong. Practical work often throws up difficulties you were not expecting. If that happens, you need to change your plans and find another way to do the job. That is not a problem, as long as you record what you changed and why.

1 PRODUCTION PLANS

The production plan is designed to help you plan your time, activities and sequences needed to design and make your product. It is your guide through the whole project. You start with the design brief and then move on to the next stage until you reach the end of the project.

In the previous chapter, production planning was explained; now you need to consider how you use a product plan to make a product.

The designer should provide the manufacturer with all of the information about the operations to be carried out and the flow of processes needed to manufacture the product. It is the job of the manufacturer to work out how the processes are to be completed.

The manufacturer will study the information in the operation process chart and flow process chart and then develop job cards or operation sheets that detail each process to be involved in manufacturing the item.

To work out how long a particular operation should take, an operator is often timed as they work on the task. This can then be used as a rough guide to how long it will take to carry out the same operation when the product is being manufactured. This information is then used by the machine operators to set up the process and carry out the activities. All the necessary information should be included to enable a worker to make the part to the specification set by the designer.

ACTIVITIES

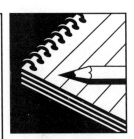

1. Design a set of job cards for your production plan. Give them to someone else to look at and see if they can follow them.

2. Carry out the task set by the job card, following the instructions precisely, and evaluate the end product against the original design.

PORTFOLIO NOTES

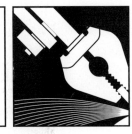

Your job cards should go into your portfolio, along with evidence that you tested them as the activity suggests.

Schedule for Manufacture

In recent years, many companies have developed new products through a team approach. This approach typically involves the marketing department and a research and development department generating product ideas, concepts and prototypes. These are then tested in selected target markets. Production engineers and advertising experts are brought in later.

The development process can take anything from 18 months to several years before a product is launched. Because of the short life cycles of many products and because of competition, the time between product conception and product launch must be as short as possible.

Many companies now take an approach that uses the skills of all departments at the earliest stages of product development. This has reduced the time it takes to develop and launch new products to less than one year.

However product ideas are generated, they need to be screened before the next stage of development can begin. Screening eliminates product ideas with low potential according to four specific criteria:

- marketability
- technical feasibility
- manufacturing feasibility
- financial feasibility.

This is often called a feasibility study.

Once all these criteria have been resolved the product will be ready for manufacturing.

A detailed and cost-effective approach is adopted for scheduling the manufacturing process. As mentioned earlier, the whole factory may need to be redesigned to cope with the processes needed to make the product. The plant layout is carefully organized so that materials are moved directly from one operation to the next, and so that they are moved as short a distance as possible.

The manufacturing team may be involved in assessing the efficiency of the manufacturing process. This may involve a diagram of the workspace and drawing in the movement of the materials around the space. This technique can be used to show where potential problems may occur, such as bottlenecks, where lots of materials are trying to get to the same place, into a store area for example.

ACTIVITIES

1. Write out a schedule for manufacturing one of your product ideas. Try to include as much detail as you can.

2. Produce a floor plan of your workspace and add to it the flow of materials. Explain whether you consider it to be an efficient flow, or whether improvements could be made.

KEY WORDS

Screened   looked at carefully

Feasibility study   looking at a product idea in the early stages to see if it is worth going any further

Bottleneck   think of the neck of a bottle; it is the narrowest part, so it is an area where the movement of things may be delayed – like a traffic jam

PORTFOLIO NOTES

Add the schedule and floor plan you produced in the activities.

Applying Quality Control Techniques

In manufacturing a product, it is important to ensure that quality control techniques are applied to each stage. Checkpoints must be well organized to make sure that a product that has dropped below an acceptable quality can be spotted and picked out of the production line, to either be reworked or scrapped.

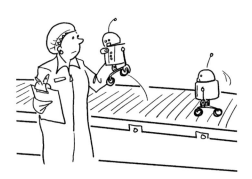

Fig 2.1 Quality control checking is an important part of the production process

Many manufacturers will also monitor:

→ humidity

→ dust

→ temperature, which may need to be controlled in the manufacturing areas.

Quality assurance systems require testing to be carried out at each major step in the manufacturing process. In addition, precise inspections should be conducted after final assembly. For example, after the products are processed, their characteristics are measured to gauge the accuracy of each process. A short-term endurance test could be carried out on each product. These tests allow the manufacturers to assure the reliability of their products.

After a product is assembled, they could then ensure the quality of the product by conducting further tests. However, this depends on the product. It is relatively easy to check that a television is working as required, but it would not be possible to test every biscuit that a company made.

These quality control techniques will involve the following:

- education and training – educate and train all personnel in every division so they can produce reliable, quality products and understand why quality is so important.

- inspection and calibration – all measuring devices used in the manufacturing process must undergo regular inspection.

- manufacturing control – many manufacturers have developed internal standards to cover such things as:

  → materials testing

  → manufacturing conditions

  → inspection methods and other operations.

The actual test carried out will vary with the product, and many specialist techniques may be used. Welded joints may be inspected, by using X-rays or special dyes, to check that they are not cracked. Poor welding might cause a pressurized component to explode. Parts for the aerospace and nuclear industries would be subject to a very high level of inspection before they could get certificates which would allow them to be used. These would be issued by independent inspection authorities.

ACTIVITIES

1. Produce a list of important points in the manufacturing process where quality checks should be carried out.

2. Describe in detail the checks that should be performed at each stage.

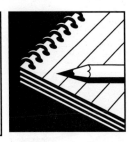

KEY WORDS

Inspection   checking to see if a product is up to standard

Inspection Authority   a professional body, independent of both the client and the manufacturer, which carries out inspections

Calibration   checking that a measuring tool or weighing scale is measuring accurately

Humidity   how much moisture is in the air

PORTFOLIO NOTES

Make a chart of where quality checks are to be included in your production process and what checks you will use.

Allow time in your production plan for some rectification to put right any faults.

Recording and Responding to Quality Data

These days, most quality data is stored in computer databases. These databases vary in their design, efficiency, and the care with which they are implemented and maintained. Procedures should be put in place to make sure that the quality data is entered at the appropriate time and that it is coded properly. The data must accurately reflect the products, places, dates and actions that it was designed to measure.

No data is ever perfect, but some data sources are more reliable than others. When checking for defects and how these may be corrected we rely on the information being input accurately. Manufacturers will look closely at quality control data over a period of time to make sure that if there are any problems these are rectified and eliminated.

Data can be obtained from operators taking measurements or noting the output from a particular process. The data could be recorded electronically using sensor and monitoring equipment.

All of this data needs to be recorded and acted upon, perhaps by making adjustments to the production process.

Sometimes the quality data can inform the manufacturer that the processes are working better than expected. This could mean that production speed is increased, or certain processes are altered.

ACTIVITY

What sort of data might be produced by a quality control system? How would you build this into a database? What reports would you want to produce from the information?

PORTFOLIO NOTES

Design a system for recording your quality checks. Remember to include space for listing what action has been taken if a quality check produces data that was not expected.

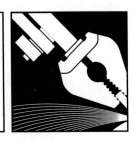

Production Control Procedures

When a product is being produced, workers will look for faults and products that are out of tolerance. These actions will ensure that a faulty product will be identified and withdrawn from the process. Sometimes the product can be rectified, but at other times it will have to be scrapped. Quality systems need to be in place in order to ensure that customers come back to buy more of the products and to save the manufacturer money.

The quality guidelines below are examples of guidelines for workers on an assembly line.

- 'Procedures for handling the reworking of retained products shall be documented in the quality control company guidelines.' That means that if a project fails inspection, the guidelines must say whether it can be reworked or must be scrapped.

- 'The guidelines and procedures must ensure that a reworked product is handled properly and will not result in it being rejected again.' Nobody wants to do the reworking twice.

- 'Additionally, when a reject occurs, the workers must identify and document corrective actions taken to prevent future occurrences that are similar in nature.' It is important to learn from mistakes and try to stop the same problem happening again.

- 'A copy of the corrective action must be provided to the manager.' Careful records of reworking must be kept.

Equipment

- The plan for the line must describe and identify the type of equipment, materials and solutions used to monitor quality control points.

- The workers will need to follow documented procedures to control, calibrate, and maintain inspection, measuring, and test equipment.

Records

- Records must be completed and maintained in order to show that quality checks are being carried out properly.

- Worksheets must contain a number and date so that they can be identified easily.

- Records of all customer complaints about the product should be kept.

- Most companies have a system of quality circles where workers can report quality concerns to the management.

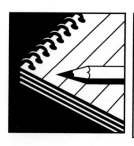

ACTIVITIES

1. Produce a document outlining the procedures that all workers must follow, if you were to employ them to make your product.

2. How would you ensure that the workers did their quality control work correctly?

KEY WORD

Production control controls that are in place to make sure the production runs smoothly

PORTFOLIO NOTES

Include your quality procedures document.

② TEAMWORK

Many companies have come to realise that staff working as part of a team are much more efficient. Team workers feel more loyalty to their fellow staff and the company.

What Makes an Effective Team?

Many studies have been carried out in order to work out what makes an effective team. It might involve the quality of the management and how important they feel the team is to the success of the operation. Football teams that lose lots of matches often get rid of the manager. Unfortunately companies that do not perform well often have to keep the manager and sack the staff!

Building a Team

The main tasks for a team leader might be:

- to define what has to be done

- to plan for quality improvement

Fig 2.2 These are all team players

- to identify problems
- to decide what steps are needed to solve the problem
- to monitor planning and production
- to encourage team members.

Improving the quality of services is best done with teams that get involved and are flexible about what they can do. The team members have specific responsibilities and want to provide excellent service to the user. These teams are sometimes formed to solve specific problems on a temporary basis or they may be a permanent solution.

The European Space Agency is made up from a number of teams that work across many scientific disciplines and international boundaries. Some of the staff may be members of a number of different teams. Although some of the teams are set up for short periods of time, a few weeks or months, many of the teams work together for up to 20 years, as the projects they work on last that long.

A work team is a group of people that come together to do a particular job. They share experiences and ideas, while respecting and supporting each other. Team members work together and communicate with each other even though they have different duties and functions and are at different levels in the organization. Teamwork groups require time to be set aside from their other duties in order to develop team strengths.

A team will need to decide how it will go about sharing ideas, perhaps in formal meetings or in brainstorming sessions, where anyone can say anything. Team members will not always agree, and the team needs to find a way of resolving conflicts so that they can reach decisions about what to do.

Characteristics of an Effective Team

- Team members share the leadership roles.
- The team develops its own work schedules and commits to the time allotted to do the work.
- Team members all take responsibility for the products they produce.
- Performance is based on achieving team products.
- Problems are discussed and resolved by the team.

There are several ways in which a supervisor can help managers and staff to become a strong team.

- Establish objectives together: define performance objectives with the team and make sure that all team members understand the objectives and what actions will need to be taken to achieve them.

- Encourage staff to suggest ways to improve services. Listen to their ideas and acknowledge their points of view. Encourage team members to discuss issues and to find solutions together.

- Have all team members actively contribute to the meeting and explain the ways in which they can participate.

- Hold meetings with the whole team during supervisory visits: discuss objectives and encourage the team to discuss their concerns.

- Organize the team: define roles and responsibilities together. If everyone has a clear role, individuals will be less likely to become frustrated and will be more willing to work together. Agree on who will assume leadership roles for different team activities.

- Explain the rules: discuss the rules, explain why they exist and discuss their implications in day-to-day practice.

- Promote team responsibility: encourage members of the team to take responsibility for completing specific tasks and to solve problems as a team. Introduce rewards only if the entire team meets objectives.

ACTIVITY

Have you worked as a member of a team? You probably have at some time in your life, at school or in clubs. What can you remember about being part of a team? Write down your thoughts and compare them to the statements in this chapter.

KEY WORD

Team   a group of people working together to achieve their objectives

PORTFOLIO NOTES

You will probably manufacture your product yourself, but do you think it would need to be manufactured by a team if it went into full production? If so, how do you think the team roles would be allocated?

PREPARING MATERIALS, COMPONENTS, INGREDIENTS, TOOLS, EQUIPMENT AND MACHINERY

3

Before starting to manufacture the product, everything must be made ready for production. Materials will have been delivered by the suppliers, and will now need preparing for use. They are removed from the store and cut to required sizes or shapes.

All components or ingredients need to be delivered to the appropriate workplace. Tools and equipment are checked and made ready for use.

The production run can now begin. The first run is always monitored extremely closely, so that all of the expected control points are in the right place and the product develops as expected.

Often the first run is a trial to produce a small batch of the product, so that the manufacturer can carry out a number of tests and checks at the end of the run, to ensure that everything has been done to the expected standards.

If all the tests are passed satisfactorily, the production run is restarted. If there have been any errors, or

mistakes made, the machines and equipment will need to be reset, or processes reorganized. It may also mean retraining, or reassigning, staff. Obviously all of this costs money, so it is important that the production planning and schedule for manufacture is accurately drawn up.

Some manufacturing companies keep a batch of products back after they have been made, as a control sample – these are used to show what the finished product was like at certain times.

Many food manufacturers keep batches of each item until well past the use-by date, so that if there are any complaints from customers they can open the batch and see what has happened to their stock. If the complaint was that the food was stale, yet the control batch was still fresh, the manufacturer would know that the purchased goods had not been stored correctly, or that the packaging had been opened.

ACTIVITIES

1. Work through your production plan and schedule for manufacture and check that it is complete.

2. Run through some of the processes and test the results. Did the outcome match with your expectations?

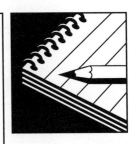

KEY WORD

Trial run   the production of a small number of components to see how the system works

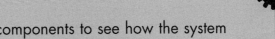

PORTFOLIO NOTES

Keep a careful note of the results of your initial tests on your product and any changes you make.

Appropriate Use of Machines

In many manufacturing environments there may be a choice of different machines or pieces of equipment that could be used to carry out particular operations. It is important that the right machine is chosen for the job.

When selecting machines, consideration should be given to:

- the operation
- the worker
- the set-up
- the workspace
- access to the workspace
- the work height
- the correct tool size.

All of these factors affect the efficiency of the machine and its capacity to do the task required.

Every machine must be examined before each use. Employees responsible for the machine and the workers using the machines should be taught how to check equipment so that worn or damaged items can be repaired or removed from service.

Machines that should be removed from service include:

- lathes/mixers with cracked or worn jaws
- pillar drills with broken bits, faulty chucks or weak, loose or broken handles
- power hammers with loose heads or a chipped striking surface
- dull band and radial saw blades
- frayed cords, broken plugs or switches or damaged extension cords.

It is essential that even fully-trained operators still follow all the manufacturer's recommended procedures when using machines and always use the proper protective equipment. Many people think that they are good enough at a particular operation to not need protection, but they are wrong. Accidents don't care how skilled a person is! If operators choose not to wear the protective equipment and then get hurt, they are responsible, not the company.

KEY WORD

Selecting   choosing a machine to use taking all relevant factors into account

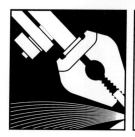

PORTFOLIO NOTES

Carry out a safety inspection of all of the equipment you will use to manufacture your product. Record your findings in a log. Report anything you feel needs acting upon.

Correct Use of Hand and Power Tools

The safest tool is the one made for the job, and used as designed. At work, tools are only to be used in the ways intended by the manufacturer. 'Creative' use, or misuse, of tools often leads to injury or a damaged product. For example, an adjustable wrench can tighten a nut, but it would be better to use a box-end wrench or a socket wrench of the proper size. Ergonomically-designed tools, of course, provide the best fit for the employee and the job.

To avoid a hazard when using hand and power tools select the right tool. When selecting a tool, the same considerations apply as when selecting a machine. Tools must always be kept in good condition, following the manufacturer's guidelines. Every tool should be examined before it is used. Employees should be taught how to check equipment so that worn or damaged items can be repaired or removed from service.

Tools that should be removed from service include:

- wrenches with cracked or worn jaws
- screwdrivers with broken bits (points) or broken handles
- hammers with a loose head or chipped striking surface
- dull saws, saw blades, and drill bits.

Follow all labels and manufacturer's recommendations when using tools, and always use the proper personal protective equipment. Store tools in a safe place, either in the work area or in a common toolbox or rack. Proper storage will mean the tools are less likely to be damaged.

Employees' Responsibilities

Employees should be responsible for:

- selecting the proper tool for the job
- checking to ensure that the tool is in good working condition
- using the tool correctly, including proper use of personal protective equipment such as safety spectacles
- cleaning and storing the tool properly.

Supervisors' Responsibilities

Supervisors should be responsible for:

- explaining the job to the employee
- providing adequate training for any tools used
- supplying protective equipment and explaining the need to use it
- ensuring that the correct tools are available
- arranging regular maintenance checks.

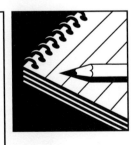

ACTIVITIES

1. Ensure all tools are stored safely when not in use – produce a set of rules for using tools.

2. Design a tool storage area that protects the tools and makes it easy to check if any are missing.

KEY WORD

Recommendations   most tools with come with manufacturer's instructions about use, maintenance and storage

PORTFOLIO NOTES

Produce a maintenance cycle for the tools you will be using for the manufacture of your product.

Tools, Equipment and Computer-Aided Manufacture

CAE (computer-aided engineering) is a broad term used by the electronic design automation (EDA) industry for the use of computers to design, analyse, and manufacture products and processes. CAE includes CAD (computer-aided design), the use of a computer for drafting and modelling designs, and CAM (computer-aided manufacturing), the use of computers for managing the manufacturing processes.

All manufacturers rely on tools and machines to produce their goods. Whether these machines are operated by workers or are automated (CAM), they need to have the correct tools in order to cut, turn, press or drill.

The tool needs to be set for speed, angle, depths, widths and so on. These must be in place before

Fig 2.3 An automated (CAM) machine

production can take place. CAM is widely used on mass-produced products made from all materials. Some machines may have several tools fitted that are loaded automatically by the computer system when they are needed in the process.

Setting up tools for a production line is a skilled job. Some tools are now being manufactured by CAM in stereo lithography systems, which create the tools from a computer drawing.

Before any tool is set up, machine safety has to be checked. The cost of tooling a machine needs to be considered and added to the cost of production.

Each production process has its own specialized equipment and tools, which may be expensive to buy or set-up. The set-up process will take time and skill, but, once a production line is set up, it should be able to run for long periods of time, providing it is properly maintained.

Maintenance is a critical issue in manufacturing. A factory will often have a maintenance team that can work on all the equipment, from fixing broken machines to repairing filing cabinet drawers! However, with the increased complexity of many machines and processes, many companies also 'buy in' maintenance from the machine makers. This may take the form of on-line support, as many of the machines now use some form of computer software to control them. The machine company may just dial in, via a modem, and check the set-up without actually having to visit the site.

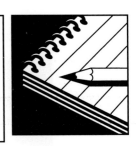

ACTIVITY

Make a list of six manufactured products: the products could be food, clothing furniture or fabric. Try to work out if their manufacture involves a machining process, and what the machine has to do with the material in order to produce the item. For example is it pressed, turned, stamped or welded?

KEY WORDS

CAD   computer-aided design

CAM   computer-aided manufacture

Tool   the part of the machine that does the shaping or joining; it might be a drill bit or a turning tool for a lathe

PORTFOLIO NOTES

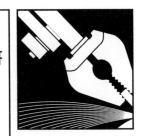

Will your product use any machine processes? If so, you need to plan them carefully. If you have CAD/CAM facilities, it will help you set many of the feed rates, cutting depths, etc. If not, you will need to do these by hand, but get them checked carefully as it can be dangerous to get them wrong.

Include your machining processes in your job cards.

Preparation, Processing and Assembly Stages

Before any product can be manufactured certain things need to be done.

- The production line must be prepared.
- The raw materials must be in place.
- The work force must be trained and know how to deal with the nature of the production run.

If the product is complex, such as a prepared meal, there will almost certainly be a range of processes that have to be gone through, up to the final packaging stage. If these are not worked out in the right sequence then the food will be spoilt.

The timing of different stages of assembly has to be planned. For example, a hot metal part will not fix to a plastic part until it is cold and cleaned.

Project management software may be used to plan the schedules.

There are certain points in the production of most multi-part products where timing is vital for the success of the product. This is called the critical path, and any delay will hold up the whole production process.

A good example of this is the assembly of a motorcar as it goes along the assembly line. Each part must be ready to fit into the next; any delays or faults in sequencing will cost time and money.

Fig 2.4 An automated vehicle production line

Usually the sequence works like this:

1. body parts pressed
2. body parts assembled
3. body parts sprayed and protected
4. mechanical parts installed
5. electrical parts installed
6. glass installed
7. interior installed
8. wheel and tyres installed
9. testing
10. quality control
11. correction
12. finish.

As mentioned at the beginning of the book, it is important that the sequencing of each stage is carefully worked out. The designer will have generated the production plan, the flow sheets will have been developed and the job cards made up. The manufacturer now needs to make sure it all goes together.

A schedule for manufacture is drawn up, listing all of the procedures, in order, with the associated job cards, and quality control procedures. Then workers or equipment can be assigned. Each process is timed and the total production time is recorded. The schedule is used to govern all of the operations that are to be carried out throughout the manufacturing process.

ACTIVITY

Look up project management software on the Internet. How does it help managers allocate equipment, materials and people? What types of report can it produce?

KEY WORDS

Preparation   getting things ready

Processing   producing the individual parts

Assembly   putting the parts together

PORTFOLIO NOTES

Produce a schedule for the manufacture of your product. Write down each stage, and include expected timings.

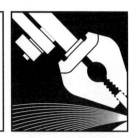

APPLYING QUALITY CONTROL 4

The purpose of quality control is to ensure, in a cost efficient manner, that the product sent to the client meets the specification. Inspecting every product is costly and could not be justified in most cases, but delivering faulty components is not going to please the client and must be avoided.

Statistical quality control is the process of inspecting enough products from given lots to generally ensure a specified quality level. The sample is checked at regular intervals in the production line. Bigger samples cost more but ensure higher quality levels.

Some quality control methods use random sampling to check a sample from the production line; in printing, for example, visual checks are made during the run. For bottle-making, visual controls are still used to check for defects. In the food industry, workers will visually check food items and manually remove defective food from the belts as it goes past.

Fig 2.5 Quality control is important

Automated checking devices using sensors are also commonly used, to check for leaks or breakages. At the end of the production line more complex products are manually checked and approved: cars, TVs and many electrical goods are checked in this way.

There are also safety checks carried out that help ensure quality. The reasons vary depending on what is being produced. In food production, the finished item is often passed through a metal detector. We do not eat metal, so if any is detected it means there has been a problem on the production line: maybe a machine part has become loose and fallen into the food.

All quality control systems are only as good as the monitoring system. If faults are noted, but nothing is done to rectify them, there is no point in noting them.

When the space shuttle blew up in 1986, it was because of the failure of a relatively inexpensive component. If quality methods had been followed and identified risks had been addressed as they should have been, this might not have happened.

ACTIVITIES

1. Investigate a range of manufactured items and see if you can locate the quality control (QC) labels. Record what information they have on them and why.

2. Explain why quality control sometimes fails.

KEY WORD

Quality control   systems put in place to make sure the quality of the product does not fall below an acceptable level. This does not necessarily mean every component will be perfect.

PORTFOLIO NOTES

Include a list of quality control checks to be made on your product. Include spaces to record the results, then you can fill in what happens when the test takes place.

5 HEALTH, SAFETY AND HYGIENE

Risk Assessment: Caring for Yourself and Others in the Workplace

Risk assessment is about examining the workplace and looking for things that could harm workers. Employers have a duty of care to their employees, which means they have to take sensible precautions to stop employees becoming ill or being injured.

How to Assess the Risks

Risk assessment may seem a complicated system, but it is mostly about applying common sense with a bit of specialist knowledge. To carry out a risk assessment, you need to do the following.

1. Look for any hazards.

2. Decide who might be harmed and how.

3. Evaluate the risks and decide whether the existing precautions are adequate or whether more should be done.

4. Record your findings.

5. Train the workers to deal with any remaining risk.

6. Review your assessment and revise it if necessary.

For most firms in the commercial service and light industrial sectors, the hazards are few and simple. Checking them is common sense, but necessary. Managers probably already know whether, for example, they have machinery that could cause harm, or if there is an awkward entrance or stair where someone could be hurt. The management then needs to consider what reasonable precautions could be put in place to avoid injury.

Small firms can do the assessment themselves; they don't have to employ a health and safety expert. A larger firm may ask a responsible employee, safety representative or safety officer to help them.

A hazard is anything that can cause harm, for example:

- processes using chemicals

- electricity

- working from ladders.

Risk is the chance, high or low, that somebody will be harmed by the hazard.

People who should be considered when carrying out risk assessment are not just the normal workforce. Everyone who has access to the workplace must be thought about:

- young workers

- trainees

- new and expectant mothers, or anyone who may be at particular risk

- cleaners

- visitors

- contractors

- maintenance workers, etc. who may not be in the workplace all the time

- members of the public, or people you share your workplace with, if there is a chance they could be hurt by your activities.

ACTIVITY

Do a risk assessment yourself, walk around your workplace and look at what could reasonably be expected to cause harm.

KEY WORDS

Hazard something that could cause harm, such as a chemical, a machine tool or even a pair of scissors

Risk the chances of the hazard causing injury and the possible severity if it does

Precaution a safety measure designed to reduce or remove the risk

PORTFOLIO NOTES

Collect manufacturers' instructions or data sheets that list safety considerations for the components, ingredients and materials that you will be using.

Recording Your Findings

If a company has fewer than five employees, they do not need to write anything down, although it is useful to keep a written record of any assessments that are carried out.

A company employing five or more people must record the findings of the risk assessments. This means writing down the hazards and deciding what is to be done to minimize the risk, such as:

• electrical installations: insulation and earthing checked

• fumes from painting: local exhaust ventilation provided and regularly checked.

The written record must be kept for future reference. If an accident does occur the management can then prove that they had done everything they could to make the environment as safe as possible. Management can also train staff to keep an eye on particular hazards and precautions and remind them regularly what those might be, perhaps with wall posters.

There are a number of places that can help with assessing risks. Anybody carrying out a risk assessment should look for advice from suppliers and equipment manufacturers.

As with all quality procedures, risk assessments should be reviewed regularly. Some changes to the workplace are bound to happen during the manufacture of a product – this means that a new set of risk assessments should be considered. It is not always necessary to re-do the assessments, but they must be reviewed. If there is any significant change, change the assessment to take account of the new hazard.

Risk assessment is not designed to stop jobs being done, merely to make the environment safer. Activities such as firework production are incredibly dangerous if the proper precautions are not carried out, but people are often hurt by much simpler hazards, such as slippery floors.

Fig 2.6 The production of fireworks could be extremely hazardous

ACTIVITIES

1. Make a list of the processes involved in manufacturing a product you have studied. Make a comment at each stage that records any risks there might be.

2. Describe how risk could be minimized in the manufacture of dangerous products, such as fireworks or nuclear material.

PORTFOLIO NOTES

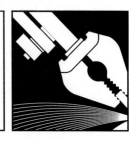

Carry out and include risk assessments for the processes you will use. They do not need to be complicated, but they need to show you are aware of the risks involved.

Safe Work Practices

Manufacturing environments are potentially dangerous. Companies have to abide by the Health and Safety at Work Act. It is essential that all staff, operators and supervisors follow the rules laid down regarding safety.

Personal Protective Equipment

Generally speaking, anything that has moving parts requires that the user wear some form of protective clothing, such as goggles or overalls. Most moving parts should be fully guarded, but even so, it is still important to wear the correct clothing.

Personal protective equipment such as safety glasses and hearing protection may be required for power cutting tools (e.g. band saws). It is the responsibility of the user to make sure that they use the correct protective equipment. In industry, ignoring safety rules can lead to disciplinary action or even dismissal. The

Fig 2.7 It is important to have the right protection when using cutting tools

employer must supply the correct safety equipment, but the employees must make sure they wear it.

Cutting Tools

When using cutting tools, normally, the direction of force should be away from the body.

Portable Power Tools

A portable power tool is just as dangerous as a stationary machine of the same kind. Because they are not fixed down, they can easily come in contact with the operator's body.

- Be sure that the power source is 'off' or unplugged (so the tool cannot be accidentally switched on) before adjusting the tool or changing bits or blades.

- Do not wear loose clothing, jewellery, ties, or any dangling objects, including long hair, which may catch in rotating parts or accessories.

- Make sure removable parts are in good condition and securely attached to the power tool before use.

Electric Tools

Electric shock is the chief hazard from electrically-powered tools. For this reason:

- do not use electric tools in damp or wet areas or in metal tanks

- only use double-insulated electric tools. If a double-insulated tool is not available, use a circuit breaker.

Air-Powered Tools

Air-powered tools require the same kind of guarding as electric tools. It is important to make sure the speed regulators or governors on these machines are carefully maintained so that the speed of the tool is constant.

Operators of air tools should follow the same principles as those using electrical devices.

- Keep hands and clothing away from the working end of the tool.

- Follow safety requirements applicable to the tool being used and the nature of the work being performed.

- Inspect and test the tool, air hose, and coupling before each use.

- Use a short chain or wire to secure all airline couplings.

- Never exceed the manufacturer's listed air pressure for the tool.

Fig 2.8 Machinery with moving parts must have guards in place – such as the protective cover over this blade

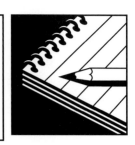

ACTIVITIES

1. Describe how to use one of the pieces of equipment in your workspace safely.

2. What types of personal protective equipment do you know about? What hazards do they protect the user from?

KEY WORD

Personal protective equipment   safety equipment designed to protect the operator, such as goggles, gloves, hairnets, etc.

PORTFOLIO NOTES

Produce a set of safety rules to be followed for each of the processes involved in manufacturing your product.

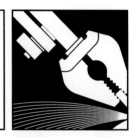

Safety at Work

Health and safety laws cover all work activities. The Health and Safety Executive enforces a range of legislation, including the Health and Safety at Work etc. Act 1974. Regulations made under this act apply to all work situations, for example the Control of Substances Hazardous to Health Regulations (COSHH) and the Workplace (Health, Safety and Welfare) Regulations.

There are other laws that cover particular hazards, such as parts of the Food and Environmental Protection Act and the Control of Pesticides Regulations, both of which are about pesticides. These and many others are specific to certain products or processes. There are also laws that cover health and safety in specific industries such as mining, nuclear power, railways, explosives and offshore oil and gas.

Fig 2.9 Special health and safety laws are in place to protect railway workers

Many of the older laws that predate the Health and Safety at Work Act, such as the Factories Act, are gradually being modernized. These cover a range of industries, but not all workplaces.

Employees have certain legal responsibilities. These include:

- taking reasonable care for their own health and safety and that of others who may be affected by what they do or do not do

- co-operating with the employer on health and safety issues

- correctly using work items provided by the employer, including personal protective equipment, in accordance with training or instructions

- not interfering with, or misusing, anything provided for their health and safety or welfare.

It is an employer's duty to protect the health, safety and welfare of their employees, and other people who might be affected by what they do. This means ensuring that employees and others are protected from anything that may cause harm. The employer has to provide information regarding health and safety for staff, and training where necessary.

It is important that safety is seen as important to all of those involved. It has been said that there are no such things as accidents: things happen because circumstances allow them to. If the circumstances around an activity are made safe, the activity is safe. Climbing mountains can be very dangerous, but being well-trained, wearing the right equipment and using ropes makes it a lot safer; a large, soft cushion to land on might help too!

ACTIVITIES

1. The above list of employees' legal duties is the basis for safe working for workers and employers. Look around your working environment and list all the precautions that are in place to ensure your safety.

2. Make a list of the safety precautions you would expect to be in place in a shopping centre.

3. Describe why there are differences between the two sets of precautions.

KEY WORD

Duties   things that it is your responsibility to do

PORTFOLIO NOTES

Make a list of safety equipment you will need for your project.

Keeping Work a Safe Place

Various laws and regulations govern the workplace. There are risk assessment and safety procedures and all sorts of forms and records that must be kept. Unless all of this is communicated to the staff, the workplace will still not be a safe environment.

A safety procedure is something you should follow in the case of a fire or other emergency. A risk assessment will have been carried out, and emergency procedures will have been designed to cope with the emergency. The procedures will then have been made public, probably with training and with notices on the walls. However, it is important that the notices are on show so that both staff and visitors can read them.

The fire procedure will cover:

- what to do if you discover a fire, who to report it to and where the fire alarms are

- where everyone should assemble so that staff can check nobody is left in the building.

As always, it is up to the employer to make sure that people read and understand the safety procedure. The employer must provide the right kind of fire extinguishers, clearly marked fire exits, and an alarm system to let everyone know when there is an emergency. They must check all equipment regularly and carry out fire drills so that everyone understands what they have to do. However, it is still up to the employees to follow the procedure.

There are also international standards for signs. This helps everyone to understand any dangers that may be present and how to avoid them.

Fig 2.10 These signs recommend specific safety gear

IF YOU DISCOVER A FIRE:

- Sound the alarm.

- For small fires use the appropriate fire extinguisher. (Do not use water or a water-type fire extinguisher on live electrical apparatus.)

- If there is time, close doors and windows on leaving.

- Inform a member of staff.

- Inform Security via extension 9999.

- Leave the building via the double doors.

- To familiarize yourself with fire and safety procedures, you are recommended to read the **Cushington College Safety Handbook.**

Fig 2.11 This sign describes a set of procedures to follow in case of fire

Fig 2.12 These signs warn you about a hazard

Fig 2.13 These signs tell you not to do something

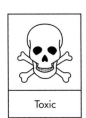  

Toxic	Highly Flammable	Explosive

Fig 2.14 These signs warn of the dangers of a substance

ACTIVITIES

1. Look around your workplace and at the materials, components and ingredients used to manufacture your product. Record the signs that can affect your work.

2. Look at the fire safety procedure for your workplace. Could you make any alterations to it that would make it even safer in the event of a fire?

KEY WORDS

Signs and symbols   there are standard pictures agreed for some dangers; this makes sure that more people understand them, including people who cannot read and also means they can be used in countries with different languages

Safety procedure   what to do in the case of an emergency; fire drills, and other such procedures, need to be practised

PORTFOLIO NOTES

What safety symbols will you need to display on the materials you are using?

Evaluating Risks

Manufacturers must continuously decide whether existing precautions are adequate or if more should be done to prevent risks. Even after all precautions have been taken, some risk usually remains. What must be considered for each significant hazard is whether this remaining risk is high, medium or low.

These steps help you to make a decision about a hazard.

- Has everything the law says to do been done? There are legal requirements on prevention of access to dangerous parts of machinery, for instance.

- Are generally accepted industry standards in place? Many activities would not be considered particularly safe, but through experience they are not a considerable hazard.

- The law says that you must do what is reasonably practicable to keep your workplace safe. Have all 'reasonable precautions' been carried out?

Once a decision has been made that something needs doing, actions must then be worked out:

- can the hazard be removed altogether?

- if not, how can the risks be controlled so that harm is unlikely?

The options would be:

- try a less risky option

- prevent access to the hazard (e.g. by guarding)

- organize work to reduce exposure to the hazard

- issue personal protective equipment

- train users to be aware of risks

Fig 2.15 Learning to evaluate risk is important!

- provide welfare facilities (e.g. first aid and washing facilities for removal of contamination).

Improving health and safety need not be an expensive activity. Putting some non-slip material on slippery steps is an inexpensive precaution considering the risk. Failure to take simple precautions could cost a lot more if an accident does happen!

More information about legal requirements and standards can be found in the HSE publications *An Introduction to Health and Safety, Essentials of Health and Safety* and *Management of Health and Safety at Work: Approved Code of Practice*. Most of these are available free from the HSE web site (details below).

ACTIVITIES

1. Investigate the statistics of workplace injuries on the Internet. Produce a graphical representation of the statistics.

2. Look at the HSE web site, **www.hse.gov.uk**. What are the most common hazards in your manufacturing area?

KEY WORD

Evaluate   look carefully at something so that you can assess it

PORTFOLIO NOTES

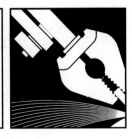

Look back through your 'Schedule of Manufacture'. Could you use any of the points above to make your product safer to produce?

Rules and Regulations for Machinery and Protective Clothing at Work

There are a number of regulations within the Provision and Use of Work Equipment Regulations 1998 that relate to workers using machinery. Employers must ensure that all workers using machinery have health and safety information and instructions about the machinery they are using. Employers must also make sure that workers get proper training to use machinery. This includes being told of any potential risks involved in their work and the precautions they should take when using particular machinery.

An employer has a duty under the Personal Protective Equipment at Work Regulations 1992 (SI 1992 No. 2966) to provide employees with protective clothing when this is required by a job. This means that an employer can insist a worker wears protective clothing if a job demands it. However, under the

Fig 2.16 Workers at a semiconductor plant wearing protective clothing

regulations, using personal protective equipment to do a job should be considered a last resort, after other ways of making a job safe have been fully explored.

Under the Health and Safety at Work Act 1974, the employer's first duty is to provide safe working conditions, before insisting on the use of personal protective clothing.

Under the Provision and Use of Work Equipment Regulations 1998 (SI 1998 No. 2306), employers must make sure that work equipment has any relevant health and safety markings, although these will not necessarily show that a piece of machinery has passed a safety 'test'.

The Ionising Radiation Regulations 1985 and the Highly Inflammable Liquids and Liquefied Petroleum Gases Regulations 1972 specify particular safety markings, but employers should use their own where there is a need (if necessary using BSI standards or in conformity with the Health and Safety (Safety Signs and Signals) Regulations 1996 (SI 1996 No. 341)).

Work equipment that requires safety marking includes: lift equipment (showing maximum safe loads), gas cylinders and containers storing hazardous substances (showing their contents).

Under the Provision and Use of Work Equipment Regulations 1998 (SI 1998 No. 2306), employers must properly maintain any work equipment and they are encouraged to keep the maintenance log up to date. This means that though employers must maintain machinery, they do not have to keep a log, although this is recommended. Properly-maintained machinery is defined in the regulations as equipment in an efficient state and in good repair. Duties to maintain machinery in this state are governed by the Health and Safety at Work Act 1974.

The Provision and Use of Work Equipment Regulations 1998 (SI 1998 No. 2306) also govern the safe use of work equipment. There are 21 general regulations, covering:

- suitability of work equipment
- maintenance
- inspection
- specific risks
- information and instructions
- training
- conformity with Community requirements
- dangerous parts of machinery
- protection against specified hazards
- high or very low temperature
- controls for starting or making a significant change in operating conditions
- stop controls
- emergency stop controls
- control systems
- isolation from sources of energy

- stability
- lighting
- maintenance operations
- markings
- warnings.

The regulations emphasize that employers are responsible for ensuring that machinery is suitable for the job, properly maintained, and that employees operating it are fully trained and informed. They also stress the importance of ensuring that controls on machines are safe and clearly marked, and that stop and start controls in particular are designed for safety.

Where an employee must use protective clothing, they must also be properly trained and informed about its use. Employees also have a personal responsibility to use protective equipment in the way in which they have been trained.

ACTIVITIES

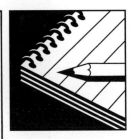

1. Collect information about the regulations listed above. Produce a short description of the points that affect you in your workplace.

2. Find out who is responsible for health and safety in your centre. What qualifications do they have for that role?

PORTFOLIO NOTES

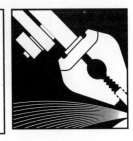

The Health and Safety Executive produces lots of guides that simplify regulations like the ones listed. See if there is one that will help you. You don't need to include it in your portfolio, but you should mention it in the safety section and list it in your bibliography.

3 Application of Technology

CHAPTER AIMS & INTRODUCTION

This chapter will explore:

- information and communications technology
- modern materials
- control technology.

The role of information and communications technology (ICT) has become more important than anyone could have predicted 50 years ago:

> There is no reason for any individual to have a computer in his home.
>
> *Ken Olsen (1926–), President, Digital Equipment, 1977*

Since the Second World War, the development of computers and computer technology has changed the world of work and society in general. The use of computers has meant that people can work faster and more reliably than they could before. Machinery can be controlled without workers. Mathematical problems can be worked out quickly. Drawings can be created and sent around the world in seconds. The computer is now commonplace and is used for numerous different tasks in the world of work.

The development of ICT has changed the role of the worker. Some companies have found that using ICT has enabled them to employ fewer workers. This can save money, as the company will be paying a smaller number of staff. However, ICT equipment and maintenance can be very expensive.

The aim of this chapter is to show how manufacturing and engineering has become more efficient. Modern approaches, processes, materials and techniques have been developed to help improve the production of goods.

ICT has been one of the major influences on modern manufacturing and engineering. ICT affects all aspects of production, from researching suppliers on the Internet, to producing working drawings on a computer screen, to controlling devices in a workshop, and in every other aspect of designing and making things. There are many books and websites that you can use to learn more about ICT.

Fig 3.1 Using technology

ACTIVITIES

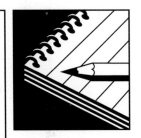

Select a product that has been developed or changed in design over recent years.

1. Describe your chosen product. Use illustrations, dimensions and any advertising you can find.

2. Describe how your chosen product has changed over recent years. You could try to produce a timeline.

3. Describe the ways in which ICT may have affected how your chosen product has been developed.

━ REVISION NOTES ━

Computers are used to:

- design things
- make things
- control things
- communicate ideas between people.

REVISION QUESTIONS

1. Choose one way in which ICT is used in modern manufacturing or engineering. Explain how the job would have been done before computers were used. Why do you think computers are now used to do that job?

2. Computers now do jobs that would be dangerous for humans. Give an example of this.

1 MANUFACTURING AND ENGINEERING SECTORS

Manufacturing sectors include:

- the biological and chemical industry
- the engineering fabrication industry
- the food and drink industry
- the paper and board industry
- the printing and publishing industry
- the textiles and clothing industry.

Engineering sectors include:

- the aeronautical industry
- the automotive industry
- the civil industry
- the computer industry
- the construction industry
- the electrical and electronic industry
- the fluid industry
- the marine industry
- the mechanical industry
- the process control industry
- the telecommunications industry.

You will need to find out what sort of items are designed and made by each of the manufacturing and engineering sectors listed above. Each sector produces a number of things. There are also lots of items that are made by combining objects from different sectors. For example, a car is made by the automotive sector. However, the carpets for the car are made in the textiles and clothing sector. The engine management system is made in the electrical and electronic sector. The braking system uses technology developed in the fluid sector and the handbook will be produced by companies in the printing and publishing sector (see Figure 3.2 opposite).

Other items may be developed within a single sector, but they may use equipment that has been developed in other sectors. For example a T-shirt will be made in the 'textiles and clothing' sector, but the machines used to make the shirt will have been made in other sectors. The finished shirts will then be delivered to shops using vehicles made in the 'automotive' sector.

It is the co-operative nature of manufacturing and engineering that enables successful products to be developed.

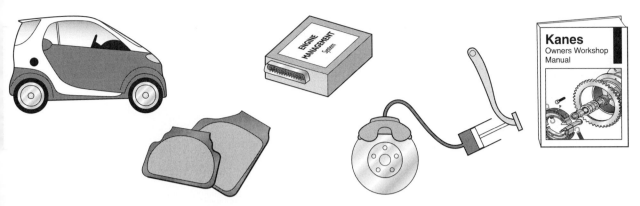

Fig 3.2 Examples of objects produced by different industries (l to r): the automotive sector, the textiles sector, the electrical and electronic sector, the fluid sector and the printing and publishing sector

ACTIVITY

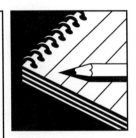

Describe the types of object produced by the manufacturing and engineering sectors. Give an example for each.

Sector	Description	Example

REVISION NOTES

You would not be expected to remember every product produced by every manufacturing sector industry, but you need to understand the types of thing each industry might make.

2 INFORMATION AND COMMUNICATIONS TECHNOLOGY

Storing and Handling Information and Data

If you look at a string of numbers like this – 8, 6, 3, 9, 8, 7 – they don't make any sense. We don't know what the numbers mean. They are data. If we are told that they are marks out of 10 for a product in a survey, we can look at them and decide that the product is quite popular. They are now in context, and have become information. We can use information to help us decide what to do.

Data manipulation has become essential in all industries. Products are only developed and made after extensive research to make sure that the customer will want the product. A specialist market research company could carry this out or, for a specialist product, the manufacturing company may do the research.

The data that is collected from the market research must be stored in a useful format. The best form of data for this task is a database or spreadsheet. Both of these formats allow the data to be organized, manipulated and viewed. These systems also allow the user to process the data to produce information.

A database is basically an electronic filing system. It is a collection of information organized in a way that makes it easier for a computer to select a particular piece of data. Databases are structured into fields, records and files.

- A field is a single piece of data – for instance, a name, or telephone number.

- A record is a collection of related fields – the name, address and telephone number of a customer.

Fig 3.3 Data from market research is stored on an electronic database for easy access

- A file is the database itself, usually stored with a distinctive name – 'customers'.

Databases are good at sorting information and searching it. They might, tell us, for instance, that a certain product is more popular with men than women. Databases can produce reports based on the data they are storing, perhaps of all the customers grouped according to which area of the country they live in.

A spreadsheet is a large table of cells. Each of these cells can contain electronic data in the form of text, numbers, and formulas. A spreadsheet is a useful format as it can perform functions on the data within a cell, such as calculations. They can be used for invoices and to analyse numerical data. They could plot charts of quality data that would make it easier to see when a product run was starting to produce too many scrap components.

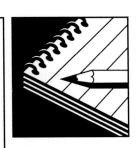

ACTIVITIES

1. Produce a database structure to record customer details.

2. Produce a report detailing how a company could use a spreadsheet application to help record stock details. Produce a form for recording information that could then be entered into a suitable spreadsheet.

KEY WORDS

Data   raw, unprocessed text or numbers

Information   data put into context so that it has meaning and we can make decisions based on it

Database   software that stores, searches and sorts data and information

Spreadsheet   software that performs calculations and plots graphs

Computer-Aided Design Techniques

Computer-aided design (CAD) has increased in popularity as computers have developed, making them more powerful and faster at manipulating data. CAD software is quite demanding in terms of the hardware it needs to run on.

There is a wide variety of CAD software packages. Some of these packages can be used on standard computers. However, many of the packages used in industry require specialist computers, with a range of input and output devices. These industrial packages are often written especially for a particular company, and are used by specially-trained workers.

Whichever CAD package is used there are certain similarities:

* there is a drawing area

* there is a library of commonly-used components

* lines and text can be formatted

* various views of the design can be seen and developed at the same time

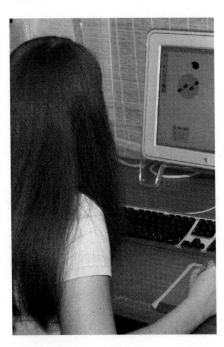

Fig 3.4 Some CAD packages can be used on standard computers

* material volumes and weights can be calculated.

The difference is often in the output: more advanced systems will enable 2D images to be developed into 3D images with surface texture, colour and simulated materials. They will also allow the 3D representation to be moved or manipulated in 'real-time'.

There are many benefits to using high quality CAD to develop ideas. These include the following.

- Rapid prototyping – enabling on-screen models to be manipulated in order to see what the final design will look like, or how it will behave in practice. This means that there is no need to make expensive models.

- Non-destructive and destructive testing – testing an object under load in order to study the object's tolerances or breaking point. Again this means that expensive models don't need to be built.

- Ease of communication – through the use of email and the Internet it is possible for designs to be distributed around the world almost instantly. This means that companies can use designers from across the globe to work together to develop the best possible solution. There is no need for costly trips around the world for meetings. The standards used to produce the designs have become international, as it is essential that anyone having to read a drawing can understand the symbols and layout.

- Ease of storage – A0 engineering drawings are extremely large and bulky to store, and a complex product might need dozens of them. Computers can store the drawings in a much smaller space, and only print them when they are needed.

CAD packages need high-resolution monitors to work well, and lots of processing power to make them work quickly. They often use special hardware, such as a graphics tablet rather than a mouse and a plotter that can print huge drawings rather than a standard printer.

ACTIVITIES

1. Produce a design using a CAD software package.

2. Produce a working drawing using drawing equipment.

3. Compare the results from the two methods of producing diagrams.

REVISION NOTES

- CAD means computer-aided design, and it involves a drawing package that runs on powerful computers.

- CAD packages can be very specialized and often use specialist input and output devices.

- CAD packages need skilled designers to work with them, but have a range of tools to make the designers' work easier.

Computer-Aided Manufacture

As with computer-aided design, computer-aided manufacture (CAM) has developed as computing power has grown. However, many of the advances in CAM have come about through discrete control systems developed for particular devices. This has lead to machinery being developed that can be controlled by an 'on-board' computer.

For example, a CNC (computer numerically controlled) lathe has the basic elements of a standard lathe, with the addition of a computer that is used to control the spindle and tool movement. This control computer can be programmed directly. It is possible to design a product using CAD and then download it directly to the lathe, in a form the on-board computer can understand. The lathe will then carry out a sequence of operations, as defined by the design, to manufacture the component, changing feed rates and even tools automatically, when it needs to.

Fig 3.5 Using CAM on the factory floor

This method of working can be seen in many different industries:

* robotic welding equipment in car manufacture plants

* computer-controlled biscuit cutters in food processing plants

* computer-controlled textile cutters in clothing manufacturing

* sheet material cutters in flat-pack kitchen manufacturing.

In many industries, a range of CAD systems is linked to a range of CAM systems to achieve an integrated manufacturing or engineering plant. In some companies this may be a number of linked plants worldwide.

CAM systems have changed the pattern of employment in some industries, because the computer takes over some of the machining decisions. It might mean that the company needs more people with computer skills and fewer people with machining skills.

The construction of a satellite and its launch rocket takes place in many different countries all over the world, with various different companies and institutions working together to produce components. The designs can then be sent electronically to the manufacturing or engineering plants, and are transferred to the CAM equipment to produce the parts.

ACTIVITIES

1. Carry out a site visit to a company that uses CAM equipment.

2. Produce a case study of approximately 500 words (include images,) explaining how the company uses CAD.

N.B. If you are unable to make a site visit, there are a number of videos and web sites that can provide details that you could use.

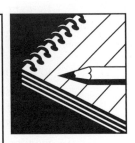

- CAM means computer-aided manufacture.

- CAD systems can be linked to CAM systems so that a product can be designed on computer and then manufactured by machines controlled by on-board computers.

- CAM tends to mean the company needs more computer specialists and fewer machinists. They still need skilled workers, but the skills they need have changed.

Communications Technology

Modern industry could not function without complex and reliable communications technology. The ability to communicate with staff in other parts of the building, off-site, or overseas has meant that production can be streamlined. This makes the process of designing and making something much more efficient.

Many companies rely heavily on telephone and email technology to communicate with their employees. This is very useful if they are working together on a project in different locations. Text messages are also useful to send short messages to workers on the move.

The ability to talk to someone in another building is now taken for granted in most modern companies. Video conferencing is also starting to make a difference to how workers communicate. Meetings can be held with people from all over the world and nobody has to leave their desk. If pictures are not needed then instant messenger services allow people to type messages in turn and hold a text-based 'conversation' in real time.

Video conferencing technology can also be used to monitor a production process. A video camera can be set up to record a machine in operation and play the video in real-time to a computer or TV screen in another part of the company. Staff can view the video, which can be very useful for training employees. It can also allow an operator to monitor more than one piece of equipment. One great benefit is that it can allow an operator to watch a process taking place

Fig 3.6 Video conferencing technology enables long distance, face to face communication

from a position they would not be able to be in normally, such as from inside a machine or in a hazardous environment.

Manufacturing and engineering companies also need to transport their goods and keep in contact with service engineers. Both of these operations have been greatly altered by the mobile telephone. Deliveries of goods and services can now be more efficiently coordinated with the increased availability of satellite navigation systems.

It is also possible to monitor goods after they have been passed to the customer, or once the goods are in use. Formula 1 racing cars have radio links that send data from sensors all over the car back to the pit

crew. The technicians can then make adjustments to the fuel or brakes without having to stop the car. Similar systems are now starting to appear in some road cars. One prestige company monitors its top of the range cars after they have been sold, and can send instructions to the engine management system anywhere in the world. It can also use the system to track a car if it has been stolen.

REVISION NOTES

Through advances in technology, employees can communicate using:

- telephone (land line or mobile)
- email (they can also attach files)
- text messages
- instant message services (chat)
- video conferencing.

REVISION QUESTIONS

1. Describe two effects that improvements in the telecommunications sector have had on manufacturing or engineering.
2. Explain why a service engineer who works on a number of sites, may feel that the mobile telephone has not made his job easier, but his manager may think the opposite.

Computer Technology

Engineers and manufacturers have found that the advent of the computer has enabled them to work faster and more efficiently. This is due to developments in microprocessor and memory devices.

Computers first started to be used commercially just after the Second World War, but they were incredibly expensive and large. In the 1970s the personal computer or PC was developed.

This came about through the use of microprocessors. These are small devices that carry out many calculations per second. Previous to this computers had used big transistors as switches. This meant that they were large and used a lot of electricity. They also produced a great deal of heat, so they had to be kept in air-conditioned rooms.

Fig 3.7 The personal computer was developed in the 1970s

As microprocessor speeds have increased, so has the capacity to store information. It is generally said that computers move on a generation every 18 months or so. This means that a brand new computer, bought today, will be out of date in 18 months! A generation, in computer terms, is a doubling of processor speed. Many PCs can now run at 3 GHz – 3 million calculations per second. In 18 months time we may start to see 6 GHz machines. However, much of what people use PCs for could be carried out on a machine running at around 100 Hz – 100 calculations per second.

Memory devices have developed in a similar way. Although memory size can mean lots of different things, depending on what it is used for, the speed of accessing stored data has increased in line with the speed of microprocessors. This means that, for a set amount of money, a computer is now faster and can hold and retrieve more information than a computer costing the same amount in the past.

This is the same for larger industrial systems. A company may spend millions of pounds on a new computer system, which in 18 months will be out of date. However, it is unlikely to be able to invest a similar amount to keep up to date. This means that the system will probably be upgraded rather than replaced.

In engineering and manufacturing this can lead to problems. As new technology becomes available, a company has to make decisions as to whether to invest in the new technology, or stick with what it has already. Good planning is essential, and it is wise to 'future proof' when you buy a computer, by choosing one that does more than you think you need.

ACTIVITIES

1. Produce a timeline charting the increase in processing power of computers – there are many good books and web sites that can provide the information you need.

2. Investigate the range of memory devices available that could be used to store and transport computer data.

3. Produce a multimedia report of your findings.

REVISION NOTES

- The 'brain' of a computer is its processor or CPU.

- Computers are constantly getting faster and can become out of date in 18 months.

- As new computers are built, they can store more data and access it more quickly.

- Replacing computers is expensive and companies will usually try to upgrade them first.

Micro-Electronic Components

Many engineered and manufactured products incorporate micro-electronics. In the 1960s, the race to put man on the moon led to the miniaturization of a number of electronic components – the integrated circuit (IC). This in turn led to the combining of these components into devices that could do more than one thing, for example, the portable cassette player or Walkman.

In the 1960s, recorded sound could be stored on tape, but not on cassettes. The tape used was a reel-to-reel system, which involved two reels, approximately 10cm in diameter, being played on a machine that was about the size of a laptop computer. As any space travel is concerned with moving weight from earth into space, the idea of taking large and heavy equipment was a problem. The compact cassette we now use was developed alongside a small, lightweight player. In the years following the space missions, this device has become smaller, lighter and able to carry out more functions, but basically it is still the same thing. The control circuitry has been combined into one IC. This has been made smaller than the earlier versions and it now uses even less power. The integration of circuitry into one device is what brought about the personal cassette player and many other similar objects.

As technology has continued to move on, there are now personal stereo systems with hard disks. These can store many hours worth of music, or any other digital data, such as video. With this capacity, some companies have developed display devices that can allow the user to view video files stored on the hard disks. These devices are designed for recreation, but are similar to devices used in industry to transport large data files securely.

The developments in display devices have meant that many machines now use a screen to display control features, or to show data from monitoring sensors. Much more data can be shown clearly using a screen rather than through a number of red and green lights, as were used in the past.

These developments have come about through the use of new materials and processes, as well as the creativity of the designers and inventors.

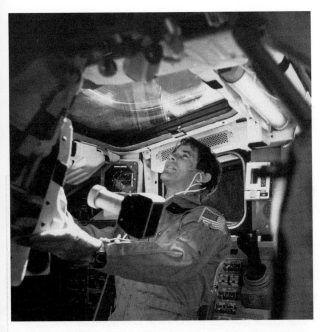

Fig 3.8 Space travel led to the development of small, lightweight electronic equipment

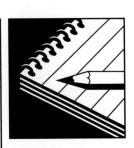

ACTIVITIES

Many personal electronic devices have become more compact over recent years. Mobile telephones have undergone a transformation similar to that of the personal stereo.

1. Carry out an investigation into the developments that have happened to mobile telephones over the last 15 years.

2. Explain how the miniaturization of the components has made using the mobile phone more 'user friendly'.

- The development of microchips, or integrated circuits, has meant that electronic devices are a lot smaller than they used to be.

- Many technologies were developed for use in the space programme, but are now being used in everyday life.

③ NEW COMPONENTS AND MODERN MATERIALS

Modern manufacturing and engineering has developed new ways to design and make things. Designers also have access to materials and components that did not exist in the past.

Throughout history we have lived through 'ages'.

- The Stone Age – when man worked with stone implements and used stone to build with.

- The Bronze Age – when man developed metallic bronze to make bronze tools and implements.

- The Iron Age – when man made things from iron-based metals.

Today we are living in the Technological Age – we can use technology to help us improve our lives.

Technology has enabled the development of new materials such as plastics, polymers and composite materials. Composite materials use the properties of more than one substance to produce a more useful material, such as:

Fig 3.9 Stone age man used implements made from stone

- carbon fibre – uses the strength and weightlessness of carbon, which is formed into plastic resins and makes the material very durable

- metallic alloys – use the properties of different metals, which are combined together to produce very strong, yet lightweight materials that can be formed into complicated shapes

- plastic sheet, plastizote, polypropylene, corriflute, etc. – the basis of these materials has been around for many years, but now they can be formed into large, brightly coloured sheets that are more durable.

These materials can be used to form new objects. To make these objects work, new components are needed. The components can be used to achieve more reliable and creative solutions to problems.

- High power, lightweight electronic power cells.

- Lighting components, such as LEDs, halogen bulbs, and energy saving bulbs.

- Powerful integrated circuits with high capacity memory chips.

- Corrosion resistant valve components for hydraulic and pneumatic equipment.

Smart materials are being developed to allow electronic circuits to be built into fibres, so that in the future a mountaineer's hat might be able to tell him when he is getting dangerously cold, because the fibres of the hat contained a heat sensor.

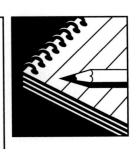

ACTIVITIES

A modern family car uses a range of different materials to produce strong and lightweight body parts. Many of these materials are difficult to investigate as they are often painted.

1. Carry out a research investigation into the materials used to make the bumpers of modern cars.

2. Describe how and why car bumpers have changed since the 1960s.

REVISION NOTES

- New technologies have produced new materials.

- New materials are often made by combining existing ones.

- New production methods can make old materials behave in different ways by changing their structure, e.g. carbon fibre.

REVISION QUESTIONS

1. What is an alloy?
2. Give one example of how an alloy can be more useful than a pure metal.

Polymers, Plastics, Adhesives and Coatings

What is a 'polymer'? The word polymer comes from the Greek 'poly' meaning many, and 'meros' meaning parts or units. A polymer is a chain-like molecule made up of smaller units, 'monomers'. The 'monomers', which are made up of atoms, bond together. This bonding makes a chain; many chains are contained in a section of material. The length and pattern of these chains and the chemicals used to produce them affect the properties of the material.

Polymers include many types of industrial materials. Polymer is often used as a term for plastic, but many biological and inorganic molecules are also polymeric. All plastics are polymers, but not all polymers are plastics.

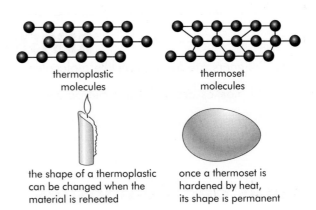

Fig 3.10 **The chemical linking of polymers**

Plastic refers to the way a material behaves under force or when it melts. Commercial polymers are formed through chemical reactions in large vessels under heat and pressure. Other ingredients are added to control how the polymer is formed and to produce the proper molecular length and desired properties. This chemical process is called 'polymerization'.

There are many different types of polymer material, and they have each been developed to do different things. Some polymers, such as acrylic, are very strong in sheet form. Acrylic is also very clear, clearer than glass. Marine centres use acrylic for the walls of large fish tanks, as they need to be very thick to withstand the pressure from millions of gallons of water. Some of the tank walls can be up to 33 cm thick and still transparent. Glass would become opaque at that thickness: you would not be able to see through it.

Other polymers can be used as adhesives as they are in liquid form at room temperature, yet when mixed with a particular catalyst they 'go off', making them hard. This property is useful in adhesives as the liquid can penetrate the surface of two materials, then when it sets it can hold the two materials together. This property is also used for coating materials, such as paint, as the liquid state bonds to the surface of the material, and then as it dries it goes hard.

ACTIVITIES

1. Make a list of five polymer materials that you could collect examples of.

2. Collect samples of each.

3. Carry out three tests on each sample to investigate:

    a. hardness

    b. transparency

    c. conductivity – heat and electricity.

4. Write up your findings as a report or on-screen presentation.

REVISION NOTES

- Polymers are long chain-like molecules.
- All plastics are polymers, but polymers can also be other things.
- Polymers can be used as solid materials like acrylic, or as glues and paints.

Metals and Composites

Many metals are mined; they are dug up out of the ground and then refined to create a pure metal. However pure metals are very rare, and are often not very useful. To make metals more useful, their properties are altered by combining them with other metals and chemicals. The resultant material is then called an alloy. Mild steel is an alloy of iron and carbon, but other metals such as chromium, molybdenum and nickel can be used to improve its properties.

By mixing materials together, the properties of the materials are combined. For instance iron, which rusts in damp environments, can be made resistant to corrosion. It can also be made harder wearing and lighter in colour. Many alloys can be recycled and the separate materials reused. A similar effect can be found in using plastic materials. Combining properties

Fig 3.11 Many metals are mined – these are pure metals

will create a substance that has the benefits of the materials it is made from.

Glass-reinforced plastic (GRP) is commonly used for small boat hulls. It is made from a liquid gel plastic with strands of glass embedded in it. The plastic resin is waterproof and easily formed, but not very strong, in fact it tends to be very brittle. The glass is used to add strength, as the strands create a mesh that holds the resin together. The two materials cannot be separated after manufacture, as they have become a single material, a composite material.

Modern developments in materials technology have led to the introduction of materials that bridge the line between plastics and metals. These often involve mixing metals with ceramics or polymers to achieve a combination of properties from the two materials.

Terfonol is a material that can be made to change shape using a magnetic field. As a magnetic field is applied to the material it can get bigger or smaller. This is dependent upon the polarity of the magnet and the strength of the magnetic field. This technique can be used to make fine adjustments to machinery extremely quickly.

NiTinol materials are metals that behave like thermoplastics. They can be formed and hold their shape, then heated and reformed, without damaging the material composition.

ACTIVITY

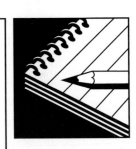

Produce a table of metals, filling in the answers to the following questions:

a. is the metal ferrous – iron-based?
b. is it an alloy – a mixture of more than one metal?
c. does it conduct electricity?
d. can it be magnetized?

Include notes on anything else you may have found out.

Metal name	Ferrous?	Alloy?	Conductor?	Magnet?	Notes

REVISION NOTES

- Metals can be mixed together to form alloys.

- Alloys are made to improve the properties of pure metals.

- Non-metals can also be combined, and metals can be combined with non-metals. If the materials are mixed, they can be separated and reused, but if they form a composite, they cannot.

Modified Food Ingredients and Methods of Preparation

Throughout history people have tried to develop ways of feeding themselves more efficiently. Modern technology has enabled scientists to find ways of helping food producers to improve their yields. Crop and animal farming has been heavily affected by a number of modern scientific developments. The biological and chemical manufacturing sectors have become increasingly important to the production of food.

Since the discovery of genetics and DNA, experts have been trying to improve the abilities of crops to defend themselves against disease, produce more fruit, or grow more quickly. This has been achieved in a similar way to the development of new alloys and composite materials. Seeds from different plants have their DNA altered by the introduction of other genetic material or DNA from plants that have different properties. The resultant seed then contains the characteristics of both plants.

Imagine one plant produces small fruit and is resistant to disease and another produces large fruit, but is not resistant to disease. The 'hybrid' will have characteristics from both: it will produce larger fruit and be more resistant to disease.

Animal feed has been studied by scientists to enable farmers to produce more meat per animal. This does not mean just bigger animals, but growth in particular areas to increase muscle density.

There are also a number of developments in the way food products are treated after they have been grown.

Fig 3.12 A genetically modified crop

Radiation can be used to kill bacteria and make fresh produce last longer. Packaging materials can be used that allow fresh produce to continue to ripen, therefore enabling produce to be picked earlier.

Once the farm has produced the raw materials (crops, fruit or meat), the conversion into food can involve engineers and manufacturers.

Much of the process of food production is now automated, or is made on a production line. The system of producing steak and kidney pies rarely involves any manual work. Raw materials arrive at the factory; the flour and fat are combined to produce the pastry; the meat and other ingredients are chopped and cooked. Then the pastry is cut and inserted into trays, where the meat filling is poured in. The top is then added and the whole pie is then passed through an oven. All of these stages are automated. The machinery is monitored by control technology so alterations to ingredients or temperatures can be carried out remotely. The finished product is then packaged ready for distribution without ever being touched by human hands.

ACTIVITIES

1. Produce a table showing the advantages and disadvantages of genetically modifying foodstuffs.

2. Investigate and produce a flow diagram for the production of a food item on an industrial scale. You may like to consider:

   - biscuits
   - soft drinks
   - bread
   - sandwiches
   - TV dinners (microwaveable ready meals).

REVISION NOTES

- Scientists and engineers are involved with food production both at the growing stage and the manufacturing stage.

- Genetically-modified crops may have better properties than the originals, but many customers are not happy about eating them.

- Animals can be bred or treated with chemicals for more economical meat.

- Organic farmers avoid all these methods.

Textile Technology

Textiles have been used throughout history. Many industrial advances have developed through the textiles industry, and then been adapted to be used in other industries. The automated loom that was designed by Jacquard using punched cards to 'program' the loom became the basis for the method of programming computers. Factory designs for the production of textiles were later adapted by many industries as 'production lines'. With modern advances in materials, textile technology has again become important to many other fields.

The development of liquid crystal displays (LCDs) has meant that, via an electrical current, images can be shown on yarns and fabrics. Until recently any display had to be mounted onto a rigid material, usually glass. This meant that displays were quite large and heavy. The development of textile technology to be able to incorporate LCDs has meant that displays can be on flexible, lightweight materials. This means that designers can build displays into different objects, such as clothing. There are a number of companies developing 'wearable' computers. The drives and processor units are discreetly sewn into the garments and the display is attached to the sleeve. There are also a number of mobile phone designs being developed with screens that are curved, or incorporated into objects such as clothing or bags.

Other uses for this type of textile technology also include photosensitive panels that can be used as blinds for windows. As the sunlight increases on the blind, an electrical current can be passed through the

Fig 3.13 Companies that make trainers will use textile technology

material, turning it more opaque thereby stopping the sunlight passing through.

Another new concept in textile design is the use of dyes that change colour when the temperature changes. A common use of this is in thermometers for use with small children. The thermometer is a strip of material containing an area that has a thermochromic dye applied to it. At certain temperatures it is one colour, but at a few degrees above or below it changes colour. This can give an indication of body or bath water temperature, without the use of traditional glass thermometers. These thermochromic dyes can also be used in clothes, for fashion or in safety equipment where the user needs to know what the temperature is.

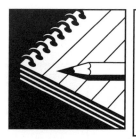

ACTIVITIES

1. Produce a number of illustrations showing how clothing could look with LCDs and thermochromic dyes.

2. Describe how these technologies could improve safety for workers.

REVISION NOTES

- Microprocessors and displays are being developed that can be built into fabrics.

- They can be used for fashion or for practical uses. A mobile phone in your hat might be fun for you but save a soldier's life.

- Thermochromic dyes can also be used for fun or for safety. They change colour depending on the temperature, so could be used to show if a person's body temperature is dangerously low.

④ SYSTEMS AND CONTROL TECHNOLOGY

Process/Quality Control and Automation

Many industrial devices now have computers built into them. These devices carry out a number of functions without an operator making adjustments. Many of these embedded computers use programmable logic controllers (PLCs). These are integrated circuits that can be programmed to carry out certain routines. One type of PLC can be used for many different applications.

The control of a dishwasher, for example, is similar to the control needed for a washing machine. The embedded computer has to make components within the machine do things at certain points in the programme. This might happen at specific times or when sensors give certain readings.

The PLC is programmed to carry out a set sequence of actions. The PLC must start a timer running, open or close particular valves, monitor temperature, turn a heater on and off and so on. The PLC is then inserted into the machine's circuits. Because the PLC in a number of devices is similar, the cost of components is kept lower. As the other components in the machines need to be able to communicate with the PLC, they are also becoming more uniform, again reducing costs to the manufacturer.

PLCs are becoming more widely used in machines and other objects. Many industrial pieces of equipment require simple monitoring and control, which can be carried out by an embedded computer using a PLC. A number of PLC devices can be connected to a master computer which can make adjustments to them if it needs to. This is a great advantage in an automated production line, where processes are repetitive. Each machine can be monitored and adjusted to ensure that the production line continues to work at an optimum level. This helps to avoid problems occurring that would stop production or cause a drop in the quality of the goods being produced.

ACTIVITIES

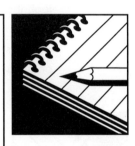

1. Describe how important embedded computers or PLCs would be to a robotic system, such as the Rover that is carrying out tests on the surface of the planet Mars.

2. If your school and college has equipment capable of programming PLCs, design and make a robotic device that uses a PLC.

REVISION NOTES

- Programmable logic controllers, or PLCs, can be built into many machines.

- They control the operation of the components of the machine, turning things on and off when they need to.

- They become cheaper if they can be used in more than one machine, because parts can be standardized and do not cost as much to make.

- Outputs from several PLCs can be fed into a master computer that can make adjustments when it needs to.

Robotics

The term 'robot' was first used in a play by Czech playwright Karel Capek in 1921. He used the term to describe artificial workers, not machines. At the time that he wrote his play, there was still very little

automation in factories. Since then factories have become increasingly reliant on technology for repetitive tasks because of the development of control systems.

Modern automated production methods require that machines carry out tasks in set sequences over long

Fig 3.14 A robot from the 1960s

periods of time. This is called continuous operation and it can create complex problems. A lathe working continuously for many hours will wear down its cutting tool. It is important that the tool can be monitored and adjusted or changed if necessary. Automatic tool changes without stopping the machine may be possible.

Robotic systems that move, such as welding equipment, need to return to a precise position after each movement. Again this will need close monitoring and adjustments to ensure that the machine movement stays within tolerances. This continued monitoring and fine-tuning of machinery makes it more likely that the items produced will be identical in size and shape. This is called 'reproducibility'. If large numbers of identical components are needed, a highly monitored system should be used. The use of such systems can decrease the time required to produce a batch of items, as the production line can work for longer periods without having to stop for maintenance or adjustments to be made by workers.

Using robotic systems instead of people can also be a great advantage when operations need to be carried out in hazardous environments where extremes of temperature or fumes and gases could be harmful to workers.

ACTIVITIES

1. Carry out an investigation and produce a report into a local industry that uses automated or robotic production methods.

2. Produce a report about the differences you can find between a company that uses robotic manufacturing systems and one that does not.

REVISION NOTES

- Robotic systems are good at repetitive tasks carried out over a long period of time.
- Continuous operation means producing goods without stopping the production lines.
- Robots can work in conditions that would be dangerous for humans.
- Robotic arms can carry out tasks very precisely but need regular checks to make sure they are calibrated properly.

ICT As Applied to Integrated Manufacturing and Engineering Systems

As mentioned in earlier sections ICT is an essential part of modern manufacturing and engineering. A product is developed using ICT as a tool to aid design, production, transport, distribution and sales.

Computer Integrated Engineering (CIE) combines the use of CAD to design products and CAM to control the machines that make them. Computer Integrated Manufacturing (CIM) covers the same areas, although the main difference between the two systems is that manufacturing is involved with making large numbers of products. This means that the equipment used is much more likely to be concerned with assembling components to produce a product, rather than dealing with raw materials.

There are many similarities in the way ICT is used in engineering and manufacturing:

- design – the use of CAD, communicating designs to others

- marketing – market research, manipulation of results from research

- production planning – flow charts, Gantt charts and flow analysis

- material supply and control – Internet sites for suppliers, monitoring of stock, Just in Time systems

- processing and production – monitoring of equipment and automation

- assembly and finishing – robotic assembly plants and the application of new materials

- packaging and dispatch – stock control, telematics to control distribution vehicles.

Fig 3.15 Robotic systems in use

ACTIVITY

Complete the table below to describe how ICT is used at each point of the production cycle.

Stage	Example of ICT	How	Example of ICT	How
Design	The use of CAD		Communicating designs to others	
Marketing	Market research		Manipulation of results from research	
Production planning	Flow charts		Gantt charts	
Material supply and control	Internet sites for suppliers		Monitoring of stock	
Processing/production	Monitoring of equipment		Automation	
Assembly and finishing	Robotic assembly plants		Application of new materials	
Packaging and dispatch	Stock control		Telematics to control distribution vehicles	

REVISION NOTES

The table above should remind you of how ICT can be used in every part of production.

Control Technology

At the start of the Industrial Revolution, machines were invented that could carry out repetitive or dangerous jobs. In recent years the development of technology has allowed more complicated machines to be made.

Manufacturing machines can now work together to carry out a number of operations in a sequence, passing a piece of work from one specialist machine to another. Constant advances in control technology have made automated machinery possible, and many people now believe that the 'worker' is no longer needed. However, this is not the case as the majority of manufacturing and engineering is still carried out by skilled individuals aided by machines.

Control technology can be used to monitor pieces of equipment, such as drilling machines. Sensors check the machine and feed the data back into the processing system. Using this data, decisions can be made as to whether drill bits are operating at the right speeds and holes are being drilled accurately. The piece of work can also be checked using optical sensors, X-rays, and ultrasound; the results will once again be fed back to the processing system. If this process is linked to other machines in a production line, a fully automated system can be developed.

One area where this sort of control system has been used to benefit the workforce and the customer is the food processing industry. Food made at home is usually made by hand, however, when companies are manufacturing many millions of food items, e.g. biscuits, each item must be identical. In many food-processing factories there is a range of control systems in operation, such as:

* refrigeration units – temperature monitoring
* ingredient transportation – conveyor systems, weight sensors and foreign body sensors

Fig 3.16 Control technology monitors this meat packaging process

* cooking – temperature monitoring, time monitoring
* packaging – weight, volume and presence sensors used in combining goods with the correct packaging.

Each stage of manufacturing is monitored electronically and results are fed back to a central processing system. Workers oversee the process and confirm the results from the sensors.

ACTIVITY

Investigate the use of control technology in the production of one of the following:

* portable stereo
* mobile telephone
* home entertainment device – DVD player, video recorder, TV
* personal computer
* kitchen units
* clothing
* food products.

KEY WORDS

Computer system   input, output, processing and feedback

Sensor   a device that senses something, such as temperature or pressure, and feeds it into a control system as an input

Feedback   using data output from the computer system to change the input; for example, changing the speed of a drill because the sensor feeds back information that the work is getting too hot

⑤ IMPACT OF MODERN TECHNOLOGY

Range, Types and Availability of Products

Modern engineering and manufacturing methods have enabled companies to produce an incredibly diverse range of goods, from foodstuffs using genetically-modified plants, to mobile telephones capable of sending and receiving live video messages.

Every sector of the engineering and manufacturing industry has developed new processes to make products. Many of these products are only made

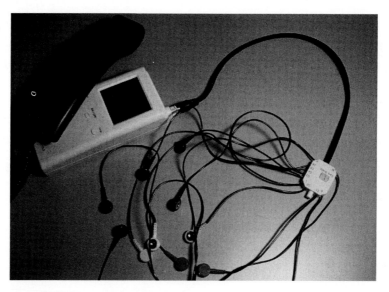

Fig 3.17 Remote technology enables the results of a patient's ECG to be sent to the hospital via a wireless connection

possible through the invention of new processes and materials. As technology has moved on, so has industry. In our society we are surrounded by goods and services that have been provided by the developments in engineering and manufacturing. These include:

- medical equipment that monitors an individual's health, remotely, via a wireless network connection to a hospital computer

- fruit which grows thousands of miles away, delivered to the supermarket in packaging that enables it to continue ripening whilst being stored

- cars that have on-board computer systems, monitoring the engine's performance and adjusting fuel use and lubrication

- personal entertainment devices that allow the user to watch full-length films, in colour, with stereo sound, while travelling

- mobile telephones that can be used anywhere in the world, even on top of Mount Everest

- jewellery that can change shape and colour depending on the mood of the wearer

- home computer systems that can be used to access the Internet, show movies or play games, as well as carry out complex business operations.

All of these use new materials or the application of new technology in order to satisfy the needs and desires of the customer.

Many of these products are commonplace now, but they are only available for as long as the technology stays available. Many of them require the use of complex new materials or processes that are themselves reliant upon other new technologies. Each sector of the engineering and manufacturing industry relies heavily on other sectors to produce successful and useful products. A shortage of raw materials or skills in one area can have a dramatic effect on other areas.

ACTIVITY

Choose a product from the list below. Produce a graphical representation of the dependencies that product has with other products and manufacturing sectors.

For example, a piece of jewellery is made using silver; the silver has to be mined and purified; the ring is then formed using machines made by another engineering sector; the finished ring is transported to the shop by road; the lorry was developed in the automotive sector, etc.

- Medical equipment
- Fruit
- Car
- Personal entertainment device
- Mobile telephone
- Item of jewellery
- Home computer system

REVISION NOTES

- Technology developments mean that new products are constantly appearing.
- Developments in one sector will have implications for other sectors; for instance, developments in biochemistry may help produce packaging that keeps food fresh longer, which helps the food industry.

Design and Development of Products

In the early part of the twentieth century a number of industrial designers got together and set up a design school. Until then most things were not designed, as we think of design now. Many of the items people used at home or at work were made to do a specific task. Products were often made as one-offs, or small batches, by hand or with machines controlled by workers.

As the century passed, a number of important things happened, including two world wars. Many great developments in technology come about through inventions first used in warfare: rockets, jet engines, portable radios, wristwatches, medical advances in pain relief, and many more. Materials were developed combining properties from a number of raw materials.

In the 1950s and 1960s, society rebelled against the dullness of the years immediately after the Second World War, when food and other items had been rationed by the government. This led society to a more optimistic view of the future of technology. USA and Russia embarked on a space exploration programme, both nations competing to get a man in space or on the moon.

Fig 3.18 This picture from the 1960s shows how everyday products have changed

In the 1970s personal computers were made possible, and most homes in the UK had cars, telephones and colour TV. Only a few years earlier these products had been considered luxuries. By the 1980s mobile telephones had appeared and computer systems were becoming more affordable and reliable. Industry started to become more reliant upon embedded computers and robotic control systems.

The new millennium has seen advances in food technology, genetic engineering of crops and the cloning of animals. Now medical engineering of replacement body parts is becoming more likely and cheap flights around the world are commonplace.

Many of the products we use now have come about through the developments of the last 100 years. As new materials and processes have become available, they have enabled engineers and manufacturers to produce more variety of products, satisfying the needs of the users.

ACTIVITIES

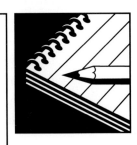

1. Make a site visit to a local engineering or manufacturing company that has been on the same premises for a number of years (over 15).

2. Carry out an interview with a member of staff who is able to describe how the facilities have changed over the years – this may be a member of staff who has worked there for many years or somebody with access to records.

3. Try to get some images of 'then' and 'now'.

4. Write up your interview in the form of a news report.

─── REVISION NOTES ───

- Over the course of the last century more people were able to buy products because they had more money.
- This meant that a design industry developed to make things which people wanted rather than needed.
- More products were made in factories, rather than by craftsmen working by hand.
- Many of these products were developed from technology originally used for something else – non-stick frying pans were developed from technology that was originally for the space programme.
- Some of the products produced are useful, some are fun and some may not prove to be popular with consumers.

Materials, Components and Ingredients

The introduction of new materials, components and ingredients has enabled designers to develop many new products, which has in turn led to changes in production methods.

The advent of modern polymer technology has enabled designers to use more complex shapes in their designs. This has led engineering and manufacturing processes to be developed to make these designs. Injection moulding is the most common method for producing plastic items. The process has been used for many years, but with the introduction of new materials, the shape of the moulding can be made much more complex, and the product can be made stronger and lighter.

Components such as PLCs, or integrated circuits, have helped miniaturize products. Along with advances in materials, this has led to many devices becoming portable, for example, the personal stereo and laptop computer. A few years ago, such items would have been too large to be carried about.

Textile technology has led to the development of breathable textiles, which allow the body to lose excess heat while keeping the wearer dry. Armoured textiles protect police and military personnel all over the world. The advances in textile technology have made the materials stronger, yet lighter and more comfortable. Motorcyclists are protected by natural materials such as leather, but also extremely strong bu flexible woven materials, such as carbon fibre.

Fig 3.19 Textile technology protects motorcyclists

Food is now much more varied than a few years ago and we can now obtain fresh ingredients from all over the world. This food can then be sold to the public or processed on an industrial level to produce high quality pre-prepared meals. The diet of an individual today can be much more varied than it would have been 20 years ago. Advances in food technology have led to a greater awareness of the body's needs. All food goods, apart from fresh produce must have a label telling users what ingredients have been used and the nutritional values of the food. This allows users to make more educated decisions over what they eat.

ACTIVITIES

1. Choose two products that you have studied and, for each product, describe how it has been affected by the use of:

   - information and communication technology

   - modern materials

   - modern production methods.

Product One:

ICT	
Modern materials	
Modern production methods	

Product Two:

ICT	
Modern materials	
Modern production methods	

2. Summarize your research in the form of index cards so that you will remember the main points for your exam.

Safety and Efficiency of Modern Methods of Production

As modern materials and processes have been developed, the efficiency of production has often increased. Automation of a production process, if carefully monitored, can improve efficiency in a number of ways.

- Less time is needed to produce a number of items, as the machines can work continuously, without lunch breaks or holidays.

- The accuracy of production can be improved, as the machine can be constantly monitored and the results from the monitoring used to make adjustments, without having to halt production.

Another advantage of modern methods of production is a more efficient use of materials.

- Computer software can be used to work out the best use for a sheet of material, working out where cuts need to be made to ensure minimum waste.

- Components can be accurately mounted onto a circuit board with robotic soldering systems.

- Stock can be monitored to ensure that anything likely to perish can be used before it becomes unusable.

- Storage conditions can be kept at an optimum state. Temperature, lighting and humidity can all be tracked by sensors.

Production costs can also be reduced through the careful management of energy consumption.

- Equipment can be monitored to ensure that it is running efficiently. If it is found to be using too much fuel, adjustments can be made to the operation or the machine operator can request a maintenance check.

- Equipment can be automatically shut down when not in use, or put in a standby mode, ready to be restarted when needed.

- Lubrication can be monitored, to ensure that any moving part does not use more energy than it needs.

Efficient transportation and distribution systems can also have a huge impact on the efficiency of production. There are very few empty lorries on the roads nowadays: haulage companies try to get a lorry to deliver its load and immediately pick up another load for distribution elsewhere, so that no time is wasted travelling without a load.

ACTIVITIES

1. Using information from a site visit, describe how efficient the production method seems to be. Try to spot where materials are transported for no apparent reason or production lines stop working because a single machine develops a problem.

2. Cars are often transported from one location to another on transporter wagons.

   - A transporter carries four cars.

   - Each car has an average fuel consumption of 40 miles per gallon.

   - The transporter has a fuel consumption of eight miles per gallon.

   a. Is it more efficient, in terms of fuel consumption, to transport the cars or to drive them to their new location?

   b. What could be the other factors that influence the use of the transporter, rather than driving each car?

REVISION NOTES

- Manufacturers and engineers are being encouraged to find more efficient ways of producing things.
- More efficient could mean using less energy or a smaller amount of raw material or a raw material that is easier to replace.
- Machines can be fitted with sensors that show when they are running too hot – a sure sign of wasted energy. This might mean they need oiling to improve lubrication.

Improved Characteristics of Products

The reliability and ease of use of many products has greatly improved due to the advent of new materials and production methods. Much more thought is put into the design of a product so that it will appeal to the customer, because there are often other products available from competitors that perform the same function.

There are hundreds of models of mobile phone, for example, each offering the same basic facility – the ability to make and receive a phone call when on the move. Each of the companies that make mobile phones has to try to make their product more useful or attractive than their competitor's version.

By using new technological developments to add extra functions, they may extend their appeal to different types of customers.

- They could make the phone smaller or lighter through the use of different materials.
- They could offer different finishes, again through the use of different materials.
- They could make the phone easier to use. This may cause a conflict with other aspects, such as

size, but through using more on-screen or voice-activated technology, companies could overcome this.

Many new products also try to appeal to the environmentalist market. There are various laws that cover the product life cycle, some of which call for any product to be recycled in some way. Many car manufacturers now offer to recycle the vehicle at the end of its life, claiming that every component will be either recycled or reused.

Many products manufactured from polymers carry the recycle symbol and the type of plastic used. There are also instructions on most goods regarding the method of disposal that should be used.

A modern glass manufacturing plant in the UK recently moved to using 100% recycled glass. Many products are available that use recycled materials, but we still have a long way to go to achieve targets set by the government and EU about how much we should recycle.

There are many products that can now be passed to specialist companies who will reclaim useful resources from the spent product. For example power cells, the 'batteries' used in mobile phones, contain various metals that can be reclaimed and then reused.

ACTIVITY

For one of the products you have studied, produce a report on how the design could be improved further, considering the following:

- size
- weight/density
- ease of use
- disposal.

The report should include sketches of changes you would make.

─── REVISION NOTES ───

- Pressures on manufacturers have changed. 100 years ago, they would not have worried about how to dispose of their product, now they have to.
- New laws on safety, disposal of toxic waste, etc., have to be taken into account by designers of new products.
- Consumers are always looking for new things, so products have to be developed to keep up, or customers will buy what they want from other companies instead.

Markets for the Products

Before a product goes into production, a company must ensure that there is a potential customer. This is often done through market research. Many products made by engineering and manufacturing companies are sold to the public, following a 'perceived need'. This means that somebody felt that a particular product would be worth making and selling as they thought the public needed it, whether they actually did or not!

Many homes in the UK have gadgets and other items that, once bought and used on a couple of occasions, are put to one side and never used again. Was there really a need for that item? We often convince ourselves that we need something when, in fact, if it were not available we wouldn't have thought about needing it.

However, there are many other products that are produced because they do improve our lives in some way. Modern improvements in medical care, such as baby monitoring devices and so on, have made a dramatic difference to the life expectancy of an individual in the UK. Modern safety equipment has saved the lives of many people. Convenience foods have enabled people to produce meals quickly, using modern microwaves and pre-packed meals.

As technology moves on, the markets for selling goods can also change. Anyone buying a television today

Fig 3.20 There is a large market for microwave meals in the UK

will probably not be interested in a black and white model, they will want the latest flat-screen, with surround sound and all the other possible extras.

This means that companies are always looking for new places to sell their goods. As countries around the world become more technological, each society's needs, or perceived needs, are met by engineering and manufacturing companies.

Due to the development of new materials and processes of manufacture, it is often relatively simple to alter a design so that it appeals to 'new' customers: Changing the words on a label so that it is in a different language, or changing the instructions on how to use a product can be done quickly through the use of ICT.

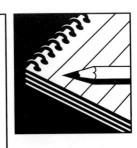

ACTIVITY

Gather information on three different consumer items from the list below:

- a mobile phone
- a low-calorie ready meal
- a piece of safety clothing or personal equipment
- a prescription drug
- a DVD
- a piece of sports equipment
- a personal entertainment device.

For each of the items, describe in detail:

- which market it has been designed for
- what specific details have been incorporated to satisfy the needs of that market
- what adaptations could be incorporated to make the item appeal to other markets.

REVISION NOTES

- If a product is to be sold there has to be a market for it.
- Markets change as consumers demand new things.
- Market research can show what consumers are looking for.
- Sometimes a designer has an idea that proves really popular, even though it didn't show up in research. This might be because the public didn't know they wanted it.
- Other times, a product that seems like a good idea doesn't sell because people just don't use it as much as they expected to. A kitchen gadget that looked useful might prove to be really difficult to clean, for instance. It might sell well at first, but not for very long.

6 CHANGES IN THE WORKFORCE AND THE WORKING ENVIRONMENT

Over the past 200 years, the UK workforce has gone through many changes. In the nineteenth century, the industrial revolution resulted in many people, including women and children, moving from cottage industries to work in large factories.

Towards the end of the nineteenth century and at the start of the twentieth century, many factories started to lose work to overseas competitors and many people lost their jobs. The wars then caused major problems in Europe. Between the wars, Europe and the USA suffered major depressions where millions of people were out of work for long periods.

In the 50 years after the Second World War, many engineering and manufacturing companies improved production and, with a strong market, they were able to employ lots of people. However, as technology improved and production methods became more automated some factory workers found that their skills were becoming obsolete. Many workers retrained and gained new skills, but some found this difficult or even impossible.

Towards the end of the twentieth century, many engineering and manufacturing jobs had been replaced by machines carrying out automated processes. As automated systems improved the reliability and accuracy of production, fewer workers were needed to service the machines.

Over recent years the UK has seen many companies move production overseas, where labour costs are lower, due to the lower wages paid to workers. These changes have meant that to be successful, engineers and manufacturing personnel have had to learn new

Fig 3.21 Many companies have moved their production overseas to places like Asia

skills. They have learnt to work in an industry that is ever-changing, where the machinery used is increasingly automated and controlled by computers. Companies now generally employ fewer, better-trained staff than in the past and the staff have to be more flexible in their approach to work.

Some companies have altered their emphasis from making to designing. They come up with ideas and designs, and then make a prototype that can be used by an overseas factory to produce the product.

Throughout this period, the working environment has improved considerably. During the industrial revolution, factories were dirty, dangerous places. Nowadays all workers in the UK are covered by the Health and Safety at Work Act, which makes it illegal to allow staff to work in a dangerous environment, or with complex equipment, without appropriate safety procedures in place. It also ensures that the health of staff is considered, meaning that they cannot be exposed to fumes and dirt that could be hazardous to health.

ACTIVITY

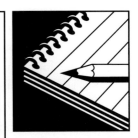

A company has been investigating different ways of manufacturing a product.

Method of manufacture	Manufacturing cost per unit	Outlay on equipment	Reject rate	Manufacturing time per unit
Manual	High	Low	High	Long
Fully automated	Low	Very high	Low	Short
Semi-automated	Medium	High	Medium	Medium
Outsourced	Medium	None	High	Very long

Using the information in the table and any other influences you can think of (such as volume of production), describe which of the manufacturing methods you would recommend to the company.

REVISION NOTES

- The pattern of employment has changed as technology has been introduced.
- Fewer people work in clerical jobs, as many of these are done quickly on computer.
- Many manual tasks have also been computerized.
- Skilled workers are still needed, but the skills they need are different.
- Most workers will have to retrain to keep their skills up to date.

⑦ IMPACT ON THE GLOBAL ENVIRONMENT AND SUSTAINABILITY

Engineering and manufacturing have enabled the western world to achieve a higher standard of living, where items that would have been considered a luxury a few years ago are now common. The increased use of the world's resources that has fuelled this development has caused some people to become concerned over whether this standard of living can be maintained.

There are also concerns over the effects of the use of the resources on the planet itself. Pollution is blamed for changes in weather patterns. Chopping down rain forests, to retrieve natural resources, causes a loss of habitat for plants and animals. Soil erosion causes loss of agricultural land. Water-borne pollution from factory waste creates problems for marine life.

Fig 3.22 Deforestation can be devastating to natural habitats

Many new materials have been developed using relatively rare raw materials. Because these materials are rare, they are difficult to find and extract. This means that alternative materials or production methods are always being investigated. However as we become more reliant on new discoveries, alternatives can be hard to find.

Modern lifestyles also require huge amounts of fuel, much of which is still derived from fossil fuels. Many petrochemical experts believe that we have used up to 50% of oil reserves and that shortages will start to have an effect on prices over the next decade. There are large reserves of coal and gas, that we could use, but they create greater problems with pollution: coal releases a great deal more carbon into the atmosphere than oil. We could turn to nuclear or sustainable fuels like solar or wind, but at the moment they produce a small fraction of the energy we use.

There are also concerns over the rest of the world developing the standard of living we enjoy in this country. The world is a finite resource; we have already destroyed massive areas of natural habitat, both on land and at sea, to produce foodstuffs. With the world's population growing we will need greater amounts of food in the future.

As a nation develops its population consumes more. This is great news for engineers and manufacturers. In the long term, we will need to look carefully at what we produce and how we produce it, to achieve a sustainable future for everyone.

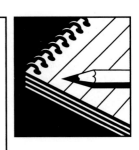

ACTIVITIES

1. Choose a product you have studied. Produce a diagram of its life cycle, from design to destruction.

2. Investigate your local recycling regulations and produce a help sheet describing how best to recycle/reuse or reclaim materials from the products you have studied.

REVISION NOTES

- Most people now accept that we need to protect our environment if future generations are to survive.

- Most people are less keen on having to do something about it if it costs them time or money.

- Manufacturers need to look at more efficient ways of producing and using energy and raw materials.

- We need to recycle more materials so that we can recover the ones we have already instead of making new ones, but this can sometimes use a lot of energy in the recycling process.

STAGES IN ENGINEERING AND MANUFACTURING A PRODUCT ⬡8

The stages are as follows:

- design
- marketing
- production planning
- material supply and control
- processing – production
- assembly and finishing
- packaging and dispatch.

Earlier sections of this book have gone through the stages involved in designing and making a product in the engineering and manufacturing industry. For your GCSE you will carry out most of the stages yourself. However, in industry it is more likely that each stage of the design and manufacture of a product will be carried out by a specific individual or team.

Some companies use external agencies to help with their projects. They may commission market research to

be carried out on their behalf by a specialist company, rather than employing staff in a marketing role.

It is relatively common for packaging materials to be 'bought in' from specialist suppliers. A design team may design the labelling and appearance of the package, but the package is often printed and prepared for use by an external company.

Wherever the stages take place, they have to be monitored and quality assurance and control systems have to be followed. A specialist department usually manages these systems: all checks carried out, and any modifications made to the product, should be recorded so that products developed in the future can incorporate any changes.

As discussed in previous sections each stage in the development of a product has been affected by the introduction of ICT.

ACTIVITY

Complete the table below stating two innovations that ICT has made to each stage.

Design	
Marketing	
Production planning	
Material supply and control	
Processing – production	
Assembly and finishing	
Packaging and dispatch	

9 INVESTIGATING PRODUCTS

An important aspect of any engineering or manufacturing project is to investigate what has gone before; it is never useful to reinvent the wheel!

Companies carry out exhaustive testing on products, both their own and those of their competitors. They tend to work through a sequence of investigations to test the product. In your investigations, you should try to do something under each of the following headings and questions.

- Research information from manufacturers and suppliers – take a look at web sites, publicity materials, and catalogues.

- Handle and examine individual products – make a physical examination of the items; take into account, size, quality of finish, and how appropriate it is to fulfil the task.

- Carry out simple tests to try to investigate the properties of the materials used, such as structure, heaviness, colour, texture, scratch and wear resistance, and areas that are most likely to be damaged.

- Evaluate the need for the technology, materials and components used. Do the materials make the best use of their properties?

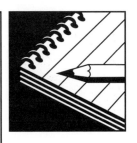

ACTIVITIES

1. Choose a product you have studied previously. For this product complete the following tasks.

   - Comment upon the role modern technology plays in the design and manufacture of the product.

   - Has the product, process or material replaced an older form of technology?

   - What are the benefits of using the technology to produce the item?

   - What are the implications of using new technology for the product and the manufacturer?

   - What is the purpose of the product? Does it satisfy a need?

   - Describe the structure and form of the product.

   - List and comment upon the materials and components used to make the product.

   - Describe, in detail, the technology used to design and make the product.

   In carrying out any investigation or test, you should write up a report detailing the following:

   - the title of the test
   - the apparatus used
   - the aim of the test
   - the expected outcomes
   - the actual outcomes
   - your conclusion.

2. Make a summary of what you found, for use in your examination.

Index

Note: page numbers in **bold** refer to key items.